# FROM THE PROJECTS TO THE
# PALACE

## A Rags To Riches To TRUE RICHES Story

# Greg Hershberg

OlivePress
צהר זית
Messianic & Christian Publisher

# FROM THE PROJECTS TO THE PALACE

## A Rags To Riches To TRUE RICHES Story

GREG HERSHBERG

Olive Press

Messianic & Christian Publisher

# From the Projects to the Palace
Copyright © 2011 by Rabbi Greg Hershberg

Printed in the USA

ISBN 978-0-9790873-8-7

1. Autobiography: ethnic 2. Judaism: general

Front cover photos and photos on pp. 49, 82, & 120 from Shutterstock.com, all rights reserved, used by permission.

Photos on page 152 copyright © 2011 by Larry Falls, Macon, Georgia, www.photosbyfalls.com

Back cover author's portrait copyright © 2011 by Denise L. Malone and Bernadette Hershberg

All other photos, including the back cover photo copyright © 2011 by the author

Cover design copyright © 2011 by Cheryl Zehr, Olive Press

Published by

**Olive Press** Messianic and Christian Publisher
www.olivepresspublisher.org       P.O. Box 163
olivepressbooks@gmail.com         Copenhagen, NY 13626

*Messianic & Christian Publisher*

Our prayer at Olive Press is that we may help make the Word of Adonai fully known, that it spread rapidly and be glorified everywhere. We hope our books help open people's eyes so they will turn from darkness to Light and from the power of the adversary to God and to trust in ישוע Yeshua (Jesus). (From II Thess. 3:1; Col. 1:25; Acts 26:18,15 NRSV *New Revised Standard Version* and CJB) May the Lord use this book in particular to reveal Himself in a mighty way to each reader.

# TABLE OF CONTENTS

# CHAPTER ONE

# IN THE PROJECTS

My father and I with my sisters at the table

# MY JEWISH PARENTS

January 1959, I was born to Jewish parents, in the garden spot of the universe, the Bronx, New York. Both my parents had their roots and lineage in European Jewry. My father's family line was from Germany, and my mother's family line was from Austria and Poland.

I would not describe my father as the typical "Jewish" dad. First of all, most Jewish men tend to be highly educated. The Jewish men that I came in contact with later in life were doctors, lawyers, accountants, etc. They were mild mannered and were usually very gentle when it came to discipline.

My father was very different from this. He was a product of the Great Depression being only ten years old in 1929. He and his family struggled very much during the next few years. Then his father died and he became somewhat responsible to help provide for his younger brother and sister.

My father got married at 20, volunteered for the military, and went off to fight in World War II as a Ranger. His first wife sent him a message that she was leaving him for another man. He had a baby girl at the time with this woman, and when the war was over he went to look for his little girl. My father was told they were living in Florida and that his daughter was sick and mistreated. So determined to find her, off to Florida he went.

He found his ex-wife and daughter and the new husband. When he tried to get his daughter, the new husband called the police. A fight ensued and my father was off to jail. My mother tells me that if it wasn't for the Jewish War Veterans, he would have stayed in jail a long time! As it was, he

11

was released from jail, but banned from the state of Florida. He came back to New York, met my mother—actually, their mothers matched them up together—and they were married.

Later, when my dad had a new baby girl, his first daughter, Merilee, who was now 17, came to New York looking for her father. They literally ran into each other in the city and Merilee asked my father if she could move in with him and his new family. My mother accepted this new addition to their young family with joy. This was long before I was born, so I only knew her as my sister. I didn't find out until I was older that she was actually my half-sister.

My father had a tough life to say the least. He was not raised in a Jewish lifestyle at all. My mother, on the other hand, was raised in a Jewish lifestyle and being part of a synagogue was important to her, so she dragged my father to synagogue each Shabbat. I was told that he never liked it, but he bore it for mother's sake as she desperately wanted me to be Bar Mitzvah-ed.

My father was a hard working World War II veteran, a recipient of the Bronze Star for bravery, as well as the Purple Heart for being severely wounded in combat. He was actually missing in action for awhile. Being raised as a boy through the Great Depression, you can just imagine how he took nothing, and I mean nothing, for granted. Because of this tough upbringing, he marinated me into the sobering fact that nothing was coming to me and you have to work hard if you want to succeed. About luck, he would say, "The harder you work the luckier you get."

He also told me, "Son, there are three kinds of people in the world. The first is a person who makes things happen. The second is a person who watches things happen, and the third is a person who wonders, 'What happened?'" He would then ask me, "Which kind of person do you want to be, kid?"

My dad worked for the United States Postal Service at their main distribution branch in Long Island City, New

York. His days were spent sorting and loading parcels for distribution. The work was mindless and trite to say the least, but with four children and a wife to support, he did what he had to do to makes ends meet. He never ever spoke about his job due to the fact that he never ever enjoyed his work.

Me in a playpen in my parents' bedroom

It is so sad that he had to spend his entire life working at a job that he utterly despised. But it wasn't about him, it was about his family.

Other vivid memories of my father are as follows. He loved to dress a little flashy. He loved jazz music. He loved listening to music by Judy Garland, Ella Fitzgerald, and Billie Holiday.

My mother, who frequently spoke Yiddish, was and still is the most unselfish, honest, forthright person I know. She has been a fine example to me of how a person should love others. My mother began her career as a social worker in Harlem, New York. Soon thereafter, she became a school teacher in the South Bronx. She shaped the minds of kindergarten age children, and taught them to love learning. She was an incredible educator, and to this very day there are students that remember her due to her tremendous dedication and devotion to their education.

My father loved my mother dearly and displayed this love frequently. Loving her and his four children was his one and only hobby. I remember him hugging my mom all the time. I also have fond memories of him grabbing hold of her, singing their anniversary song, "The Days of Wine and Roses" and dancing with her. He adored her and admired her. He being without education was so proud of her having a college degree and being a teacher. All he asked of her was that she not bring her job home with her. But because she loved her job so much, that was impossible.

My mom shared with me my dad's lack of communication. He never spoke much or shared his feelings. My dad, an incessant pipe smoker, was also a childhood diabetic. He was on insulin as a young boy, but as an adult, he was prescribed an oral medication called Diabinese. My mom said he had a secret fear of going blind due to his diabetes. Thus his diet was very healthy. He stayed away from sugar, eating diabetic desserts instead. Mom actually wasn't the greatest cook, but Dad ate everything she made and always told her it was delicious.

Both my parents were solid citizens who were so very dedicated to their family, as well as to each other. They had a real solid influence on my life, and I was blessed by being raised in a home where values and morals were taught.

## MY CHILDHOOD

As I mentioned, we lived in the garden spot of the universe, the Bronx, in a low income housing project. By the 1970's, many Jewish people in the Bronx had become affluent and moved out to the suburbs. Our family was not one of those families, so we stayed behind in the projects along with most of the elderly

My sister and I on our street

Jewish folks who had to stay because of their fixed incomes.

Our neighborhood was located in the Bronx at the intersection of White Plains Road and Gun Hill Road, and

Me in our shared bedroom

was known as the "Gun Hill Projects". There were six buildings with twelve stories each, so they were vast. When I went back as an adult, the buildings struck me as looking more like prisons than apartment buildings. It was rough and tough, to say the least. In the projects we were exposed to drugs, broken households, crime, etc.

Our apartment was small with only two bedrooms. I slept in the same room with my two sisters. My older sister, Merilee got married when I was very young, so she was already out of the house. In our bedroom we had a bunk bed and a twin bed just about on top of each other. We did not have much in the way of finances for buying new clothes and such, but my mother always made sure we were more than presentable when we went to school.

Our furniture was sparse. My dad had a reclining yard chair in his bedroom where he would sit to read the newspaper and listen to the radio. With that chair and the radio, he thought he had the life!

He also had a movie camera and was always taking pictures of us. There were six giant lights that he would shine in our face and say, "It's a moving picture, so move!" Then he loved to have us all sit down to watch ourselves in those jumpy, short, silent films.

We went to public school and we came home to an empty house as my mother and father both worked. My father took three trains to get to work, so he was up at about 4:30 A.M. I never saw him in the morning, but we always got together for dinner. My mom and dad were involved in our lives as much as they could possibly be. They played a major role in making sure we kept out of trouble. In other words, they did what they had to do to keep us on the straight and narrow.

Please don't misunderstand; we had wonderful neighbors in our housing project. Many good people lived there. We had a cross section of ethnicities—somewhat of a melting pot of nations.

We had many friends that we played with constantly. No need for play dates, nor organized sports, and what in the world was an indoor playground? We would just go outside and play stickball, hot peas and butter, or off the stoop. We were not organized, just a bunch of kids choosing up sides and playing some good old Bronx games. My life as a youngster was so very different than my children's lives today.

We had some board games, but we mainly went down the street to the school yard, or we would play in the "park" nearby. It wasn't really a park as it was all cement. It had a basketball hoop, a handball court, a place to play stickball, and a one foot deep cement pool with sprinklers that were turned on in the summer. These were the days you could go off for hours and there were no worries about pedophiles or abductions.

Across the street from the projects was what we called the "island". It wasn't a legitimate island, as it was not surrounded by water, but was a sidewalk that was shaped like an oval located under the elevated trains. In the center were some benches where my father would sit and read a newspaper as we rode our bikes around the perimeter.

My sisters and I were incredibly close. We did everything together and we looked out for one another. Everywhere my sisters went, they would take me along. It was just expected that they would do that. They helped make my life a lot of fun. I have this vivid memory from when I was young. I had these football uniform pajamas and my sisters would throw me the football in the apartment and when I made believe I scored, they would act like cheerleaders and give out a shout on my behalf.

16

I remember in the summer walking with my dad and family about a mile and a half to Carvel just to get a chocolate dipped ice cream cone. This was a highlight to me. Today people think they have to do something big, but I disagree. It is the little things that can make the biggest difference in a person's life sometimes.

So, although we were poor financially, we were filthy rich in so many other ways.

When I was a little older, my dad got us a membership at a pool club called Shorehaven for the summers. We took a bus there. It was on the Long Island Sound in the Bronx. It had a large swimming pool which we thought was amazing.

## MY DAD AND ME

I loved my father immensely. I always felt a sense of profound protection from him even when he was not around. I knew he wasn't going to let anyone hurt me. Although he was tough and physically impressive, he was tender as well. He had a very deep love for me. I was not allowed to go to bed at night without kissing him good-night on the cheek. To this day, I can still remember how his

My father holding me

whiskers felt against his lips. He was so very proud of his son, his only son, and he would always brag about me.

I loved my father so much that I had this haunting fear that he might die. I even had recurring nightmares about it.

I would wake up feeling terrified and was always so relieved to go to his room and discover it was only a dream.

As I said, I was the only boy, so my father being a man's man poured himself into me. Since he was raised during the depression, he never really had time to be a kid and do the things that kids do, so he would live vicariously through me. Because he had such limited opportunities in life, my success would be his success. I was going to be the straight A student, the star athlete, and overall, the achiever of greatness. He even had this standing joke with me. He'd say, "If you want, kid, you could be the first Jewish president."

He ingrained in me a spirit of excellence, so I always would go for the gold, especially when it came to my studies. He would say, "Be the best you can be. Strive for excellence, and do not settle for second best." I remember when I would take a test at school and come home with a 97%; my father would ask if anyone got a 100%. In other words he was asking, "Did anyone beat you?"

My father's line of thinking still resonates in my soul even to this very day. I tend to place much pressure on myself. On a good note, his teaching served me well. I ended up graduating high school at the top of my class, and I managed to be awarded a scholastic scholarship to college.

I do not remember having many conversations with my father about life. He didn't talk much. Most parents were not close with their children fifty years ago. There was a generation gap which is so very different from today. The truth is, he had a short fuse. I would not describe him as a gentle man. He would often lose his temper. We never knew what was going to set him off. Sometimes he would chase us down to give us a whack.

One year Dad was able to scrape enough money together for my mom, him, and me to fly to California to visit his mother. This was a major deal for us to get on an airplane. While in California, he took me to Disney Land, his movie camera in hand. Again, this was another privilege beyond my wildest childhood dreams. While there, Dad handed me the precious camera to hold while he bought us some food or tickets or something. The camera was heavy, so me being a typical boy, I set it down on the ground. Well, my dad could not believe I did such a careless thing. His fuse was ignited and I got it again. But, as I said, he was also very affectionate. He was devoted to my mom and us, and he was a solid provider. I remember feeling very secure in his love.

Dad was very interested in sports. I remember him always trying to teach me about sports and playing some paddleball with him. I also remember my father constantly trying to build up my body. I was born with a concave chest known medically as pectus excavatum. My father did not receive a good report from the doctors back in 1959, so he took measures in his own hands. As I grew older, he bought me pectoral cables, bull workers, weights, etc. He wanted me to be able to build my muscles because the doctors told my parents I may not be able to play sports due to this condition.

Dad also had a humorous side. While we were in California, Grandma took us on a side trip to Las Vegas, where Dad won big playing the slot machine. The bells went off and he was told he won $500, a huge amount of money back then. My grandmother got all excited, grabbing him and yelling his nickname over and over. He called a security guard over and said, "Officer, this crazy lady is bothering me."

"What?!! I'm your mother!" Grandma was shocked.

Without missing a beat, Dad said, "See, Officer, she thinks she's my mother!" Dad loved to play jokes like that on people. He did it all the time.

As I mentioned, my dad was very proud of me and I think I know why. I believe he was very insecure about his lack of education. Because of it, he lacked confidence, and kept to himself. He really didn't have any friends. He wanted so badly for his children to get a solid education. For whatever reason, I seemed to be the child who showed the most interest in schooling. Perhaps it was because my father invested more time with me than the others. I don't know. But I'm glad I could please him.

I remember playing some football on the block with my friends. They were rough kids who rarely went to school. Most of their fathers were gone and their moms worked. My friends played hooky all the time while their moms thought they were in school. Sadly enough, most of them didn't even graduate high school. They also got very involved with drugs. Actually I had two sets of friends. I had friends at school who were predominantly Jewish and were in the advanced classes like myself. Then I had my real friends at home, who lived on the same block as me and were totally non-Jewish. They were Italian, Irish, and Hispanic. Their names were Vinnie, Michael, Louie, Carlos, etc. I hung around with them on a regular basis. I kind of had this bad boy attitude but with a really good head on my shoulders. The Jewish kids weren't fun enough or "cool" enough for Greg. I was going to be a tough Jew.

My neighborhood friends didn't really know that I was smart because I didn't want them to know. You see it wasn't considered cool to be smart. Go figure? So I lived this double life—schoolboy by day and bad boy by night. I guess I really didn't know who I was.

When I would get my report card, my father would be blown away because in junior high and high school I would always get straight A's. This one particular day, my dad saw my report card and came running out in the street to show my friends. I was so embarrassed, as they finally knew. It ended up that some of the guys were actually proud of me.

Now let me say here that whenever I took standardized tests, I did very well in the math and science sections, but performed miserably in the reading comprehension sections. However, back in that day, there wasn't much stock put in those tests, so those low scores didn't bother my father too much. My keen memory helped me compensate for my poor reading comprehension. I could remember almost word-for-word what the teachers said. In the higher grades, I would read the "Cliff Notes" of the required books and regurgitate them well in term papers and essay questions on tests. Of course, this was back in the 1960's before we knew much about dyslexia, attention deficit disorder, and hyperactivity disorder. (For those who are not familiar with Cliff Notes, they are summary study guides for classic literature, and they are used by the student to bypass the arduous task of reading the entire book.)

My father never drove, but he did convince my mother to drive. She got her license when she was about 43 year old, and so we finally had freedom to come and go as we liked. We would travel every weekend to upstate New York to visit my oldest sister, Merilee, and her children. Family was very important to my dad.

Merilee had married a great guy. Dad thought she had hit it big! They lived in the country on five acres of land. To Dad, only ever having lived in the projects, this was really something. They had a small house with a little circular drive, but to Dad it was the Taj Mahal.

I also remember Tuesday evenings very well. My mother was studying for her master's degree, and she had class after work on Tuesdays. So my dad and I would go to eat at the Chinese restaurant and we would foot race home to see who was the fastest. He always won this race.

Overall I wish my father was able to communicate better and share his heart with me. Recently, I talked to my mom about Dad's lack of communication and she said she didn't even feel like she knew him very well. I am unfortunately a lot like my dad in having a short fuse sometimes, but I am able to express myself better than he was. So I can explain to people why I'm feeling upset. The bottom line is my father did the best he could with the skills he had. His love was apparent in not what he said, but in what he did!

My mother on the other hand was very gentle and sweet. She actually never hit us. She wanted me to be nonviolent, so she wouldn't let Dad talk to me about the war or the military. She was an educator, and she also was so very proud of me. She would always take me to school when I had the day off and show me off to her fellow teachers.

What I loved the most about growing up was having dinner together as a family. To this day it is very important for my wife, my four children, and I to have dinner together. I guess I loved it so much that I have continued the tradition some 30 years later. I thank God I have such fond family memories.

## CHILDHOOD ANTI-SEMITIC EXPERIENCE

Being Jewish, I experienced anti-Semitism. There were incidences when I was called a "Jew Bastard" or a "Cheap Jew". The boys in my neighborhood were so tough and scary to me when I was little. Anti-Semitic remarks frequently came out of their mouths, not necessarily just to me. They even said such insults to put each other down. I couldn't get away from it. In our neighborhood which was almost all Catholic, both Irish and Italian, there was a huge Catholic church called The Immaculate Conception. Because of all the anti-Semitism I experienced, I was even afraid of the church building itself. While passing the church one day, I peered into the open door. Upon seeing a man hanging on a giant cross, I thought these Catholics kill people! From that day forward I crossed the street to walk by.

When I was about 14 years old, I was invited to eat dinner at a friend's house. I was at their table feeling a tad uncomfortable to begin with because I didn't really know the family that well. They lived in the Bronx where the houses were so close to each other that you could stick your hand out and touch the next one. It was summertime. The windows were open and the neighbor next door was talking rather loudly. All of a sudden my friend's sister yelled, "Tell that Jew bastard next door to shut up!" I was mortified. I remember feeling sick to my stomach.

First of all, I was not only embarrassed for myself, but embarrassed for my friend's sister as well. I thought I should say something, but as a young boy in a situation like this, I was too timid. I just didn't know what to say or how to say it.

My friend piped in, "You know, Greg is Jewish."

His sister replied, "Well, he's not that kind of a Jew."

To this day, I'm not sure what that statement means. I guess she was trying to smooth things over by letting me know I am a clean Jew as opposed to a dirty Jew.

I experienced more than just verbal anti-Semitism. Four of us Jewish boys would carpool together in a taxi to go from our project to our synagogue for Hebrew school. We couldn't walk because we went late in the day when it wasn't safe. In the late fall it was nearing darkness when we left. We went every Tuesday and Thursday. Many times, when we arrived, the neighborhood kids would be waiting for us and would throw rocks at us when we got out of the taxi.

At Hebrew school, they taught us that Jewish people were chosen by God. I never understood how we could be God's chosen people and yet endure such intense, frequent, and long-lasting worldwide persecution. I do understand being chosen now.

My mother was staunchly against racial prejudice. Both my parents were adamantly against any kind of bias or judgment based on a person's skin color or religious persuasion. I am so very thankful that we were taught that under the skin we are all the same and that there is only one race, the human one! I believe with all my heart that prejudice is something we acquire not something innate in us. My sisters and I were taught to be loving and accepting as opposed to hateful and intolerant. I believe this was ingrained in my parents from Jewish thought as the Lord tells us in the Torah not to treat anyone as an alien since we, the Jewish people, were once strangers in Egypt.

I do not want to appear like I have a high sensitivity towards anti-Semitism, but truth be told I experienced my fair share. You see, I look quite Mediterranean with dark skin, dark eyes, and dark hair. (Well, that is, when I had hair as a young man.) I would be over at a friend's house, and I would hear anti-Semitic comments. When the person would find out I was Jewish, they would always say, "You don't look Jewish", instead of saying, "I'm terribly sorry for my ignorant comments." But, I guess if they knew their comments were derogatory, they would not have made them in the first place.

I found people feel it's alright to make comments like "you cheap Jew", or "let's try and 'Jew' them down". When people say, "Hey, we've got bagels for you, Rabbi" it doesn't feel loving! Recently, when I was taking a group from Georgia on a pilgrimage to Israel, one of the ladies on the trip showed me a piece of jewelry she purchased, and proclaimed proudly to all nearby that she had "Jew-ed down" the merchant. She had no idea whatsoever that her comment was inappropriate. Go figure! The fact remains that these statements are hurtful at best and those who use them should come to grips that they have some prejudiced attitudes.

There's an old saying, "Misunderstanding leads to all kinds of evil." Where do people get the idea that the Jews are trying to take over the world? When did Israel ever try such a thing? People need to stop and think about what they are saying. They need to check the facts and find out the truth.

I remember hearing all these kinds of comments fairly regularly, and yet I was never brave enough to stand up and correct people. Now I do. (I privately, gently corrected the lady on the pilgrimage mentioned above.) I now know that anti-Semitism is of the anti-Christ and the Lord hates it as well. See Zechariah 2:8.

Growing up, I felt as though there was nothing special about being Jewish. In fact, I felt somewhat cursed at times, as it appeared that the world did not have a high regard for the Jewish people or the nation of Israel. What a shame when, in fact, this rather small group of people have provided the world with so much blessing.

By the time I was 18, I was done being Jewish. I wouldn't even give my last name in order to avoid the potential onslaught of derogatory comments that could follow. I just introduced myself as Greg. Today I realize that my enemy does not have a social security number. The real enemy is satan himself. Anti-Semitism, for the most part, is born out of ignorance. Yet for the Christian community, this should never be. Read Genesis 12:3 and John 4:22.

## MY BAR MITZVAH AND SYNAGOGUE

I was raised in an Orthodox synagogue called "Anshe Emet" which translates in English as "People of Truth". Although Congregation Anshe Emet was Orthodox, my family would be considered more along the conservative/reformed ranks. Sometimes a person's daily religious practices do not always reflect what they do on Saturday or Sunday.

Mom kissing me at my Bar Mitzvah

We did, however, abide by the Orthodox practice of walking the ten blocks to our little broken down synagogue every Shabbat (Saturday). I went to Hebrew

My sister, Michelle, bringing me my new Tallit

School there two times a week after my full day at public school. I do not have fond memories of Hebrew School. I actually hated it.

Shabbat at home was fairly non-existent. You see we were not really Orthodox in practice. My mother was raised Orthodox, and for the most part we just followed suit. I believe our faith, or lack thereof, was more cultural than spiritual. "Faith" was more something that happened on the outside than the inside for us. It was more about outward ritual than inward reality. I don't really know who to blame, but the bottom line is you can know all about someone and never know who they really are.

We attended Synagogue because we felt it was important to keep the traditions of past generations alive. Truth be told, we were going out of obligation and not out of desire. We followed rules as we knew nothing about relationship or shall I say relating to God.

By the same token, God was not at the center of our lives. We knew about Him, and we had a respect for Him, but there was no "real" relationship with Him. I learned more about external religious ritual rather than internal relational reality. I had this horrible image of God. I had envisioned Him as being totally unapproachable, and as just waiting for me to mess up so He could let me have it! What a distorted and twisted way of looking at a God who in the book of Exodus says, "I have heard your cry and I am coming to your rescue."

Sadly enough, this was not my family's revelation.

Who knew that God desired intimacy with His people? Who knew that we could speak to God and He would speak back to us? Who knew that God wants to be intimately involved with us so much so that He wants us to call him Abba, Daddy? Well I know this to be true now and I will never ever let go of this revelation. I will never ever let anyone or anything get in the way of my relationship with God ever again.

I remember my days leading up to my Bar Mitz-

Blessing the bread at my Bar Mitzvah, now wearing my new Tallit

vah all too well. You see when you attend an Orthodox Synagogue you are expected to recite not only your Haftorah (the prophetic portion of the weekly Scripture reading that align with your thirteenth birthday), but many of the Shabbat morning prayers along with their respective melodies. This took years to learn. It was burdensome and at times overwhelming. I was trying to do well in school, and play some extra-curricular activities, so Hebrew School two times a week just didn't fit into my schedule. I begged my parents to give me a pass on my Bar Mitzvah, but this was taboo, according to our traditions.

Although I really didn't understand the reason for the Bar Mitzvah I still had to go through with it. Anything less was out of the question. I remember crying ferociously in the Rabbi's office, with my mother in attendance, as the Rabbi said this was the way it was and there was no room for debate or discussion!

27

So every day, about a year out from my Bar Mitzvah, I listened to the cassette tape that the Rabbi made for me with the chanting of the Haftorah Portion along with the melody until I had it down pat. I knew all the prayers and read the Hebrew very well when the day came.

I really do not want to say anything derogatory about my Rabbi growing up, but let's just say he was no game show host. He was quite serious. I never remember him smiling. In fact, I never saw his teeth, except once at a men's meeting when I saw him biting into a bagel with cream cheese and lox. He did not appear to be a happy man, but then again maybe I was just so unhappy being there that I brought the worst out of him. Perhaps it was also because he knew that my parents were not really living the Orthodox lifestyle.

The term Bar Mitzvah translates as "a Son of the Commandments". Although this is not stressed, nor really understood by many even in the Jewish faith, it denotes a rite of passage so to speak, where the young boy passes from a child into manhood. He is now responsible to obey the Lord and walk righteously before Him. Up to this point, the child should have been thoroughly instructed in the ways of God, and he is now responsible to walk it out. He is not left out in the cold, though. Rather his father and the other men in the Jewish community should rally around him and help to guide him in his walk with the Lord.

Now, this is, of course, in theory, as this is not actually how it is in practice these days. Sadly, today most of our Jewish children do not really understand the beauty and significance of their Bar Mitzvah. In fact, you could say that today at any given Bar Mitzvah, there is usually more "bar" than mitzvah.

My Rabbi, as I said, was very stern. Back in the day, Rabbis, especially the Orthodox, leaned on the side of austere. The people were not well educated in Judaism, so the Rabbi knew everything and the people knew nothing. Whatever the Rabbi said was the way it was. He was not friendly or warm. He had no bedside manner whatsoever. Truth be told, he was there to conduct services and prepare the children for their Bar Mitzvah.

The synagogue was dwindling as many of the Jewish people had left the Bronx for the suburbs. The only ones that were left were the elderly and the impoverished. There were only about 50-60 people with very few children. It is very important in Jewish life for children to carry on the traditions of the elders. Therefore the synagogue held Hebrew school even though all the classes had to be taught by the Rabbi alone. Because there were so few children, I can remember some of the old men kissing my mother's fingers at the end of my Bar Mitzvah as a token of their appreciation that my mother decided to raise me in the traditions of the elders. Never mind the fact that I was clueless as to the real reason behind the Bar Mitzvah.

After my Bar Mitzvah, my family and I began to drift away from the faith. We eventually only appeared at synagogue on the High Holy days in the fall, which would be Rosh Hashanah and Yom Kippur.

Me with my son reading from the Torah at his Bar Mitzvah

## My Son's Bar Mitzvah

I can tell you that when my son was Bar Mitzvah-ed in 2007, I made sure he understood the spiritual nature of the rite, as well as making sure that from the beginning he knew

29

the Lord's love, grace, mercy, and compassion over him. By the time my son's Bar Mitzvah rolled around, he was fully immersed in an intimate relationship with the Lord. Anyone can learn Hebrew and a bunch of melodies, but it takes time for the heart and soul to develop a relationship with God, and this was the focal point of our children's upbringing.

We go to synagogue out of appreciation and desperation, but never ever out of obligation. We love the Lord so very much and look for any excuse to spend time with Him. We look for Him the very first thing in the morning and we know Him as Father God, infinitely high, and yet intimately nigh!

I never felt the care and concern from my Rabbi that I hope I bestow upon my people here at Congregation Beth Yeshua. Then again, a person can't give what they haven't got. What I mean is how can you love someone with a love you have never received? Sadly, my Rabbi hadn't met his Messiah.

The Lord has magnificently displayed His love for us in Messiah Yeshua's bloody and sacrificial death. This is the proof that the Lord loves us with an everlasting love. There is no greater love than one who lays down his life for another. So I thank the Lord daily for His lovely love revelation that He has so wonderfully and graciously shown us!

My wife and I blessing our son on his Bar Mitzvah

# IN THE PROJECTS

# CHAPTER TWO

# SEARCHING

My twelfth birthday
with Mom and Dad

## More About My Father

By the time I was 15, my three sisters were married so it was just Mom, Dad and me. At that tender age, the unthinkable happened. My father died. I remember it like it was yesterday, even though it was 1974. One thing I thank God for is that I got to kiss him the very night before he died. That night I awoke to the sound of my mother screaming from their bedroom. At first I thought it was just another one of my nightmares, but to my horror I began to realize it was no dream this time, but a terrifying reality. I ran into my mother's room and saw my father not moving or breathing on his bed. I cry as I am writing this. The last memory I had of my dear father was watching two men placing him in a huge, black body bag and carrying him out to a waiting van.

The death of my father was devastatingly horrible. I remember feeling so insecure without him and so very vulnerable to danger. He was a protector, my protector, and whenever he was around I had no fears. When he was gone, I felt as though I lost my right arm. It was very unsettling to say the least.

After my father passed away, it was just my mother and I living alone. My mother became a basket case for a season, and with my sisters already married and out of the house, I had no one to lean on. I decided to take matters into my own hands. I devised a way to handle the situation myself. I would make-believe that I never had a father. I know this charade sounds crazy, but the thought of not having him around was too painful, so pretending that I had never had him was the best solution, as I saw it. It seems so sad to me

35

even today that I thought this was my best choice, but in desperate situations people do desperate things.

After my father died, my mom and I finally moved out of the Bronx and I ended up with a whole new set of friends in the suburbs of Yonkers, New York. This got me off of the wrong path that was leading me to drugs and trouble.

Once my father passed away and we moved, my mother and I began to drift away from practicing our Jewish faith. We never joined another synagogue. We did manage to keep the Jewish High Holy Days of Rosh HaShana and Yom Kippur and in the spring enjoyed our family get-together on Passover. Aside from that, we basically embraced a more secular lifestyle. It wasn't until my encounter in Israel that I came back in contact with the Torah.

The message that I received from my father's passing was, "Life is short, pal, so grab all the gusto you can get your grubby little hands on and remember to look out for yourself." This, of course, is not a good philosophy, for it leads to selfishness and self-centeredness. Although I never meant to hurt anyone, living for self is a sure-fire way to hurt others, as well as yourself. When I met the Lord all that changed, and I learned that it is better to give than to receive.

## ADULTHOOD

After my father's death, I began to live the party lifestyle while still paying close attention to my studies. With the level of drive that my father had instilled in me, I was able to graduate high school with high academic honors and receive a scholastic scholarship to attend college, where I graduated Magna Cum Laude.

I then pursued a career in public accounting where I found myself like a fish out of water. I was hired by Arthur Anderson and Company, a very prestigious public accounting firm in New York. I worked there from 1980-1982. This was one of the "Big 8" accounting and consulting firms— the top eight firms of their kind in the world. Just to get an interview with them, you needed to graduate with at least a 3.75 index from a quality school. Then after a series of interviews they would let you know if you got the job. Fortunately, I

My college graduation

did, in fact, graduate with a 3.88 index from an excellent college that specialized in the field of accounting.

Prestige aside, I did not like the work one bit. In fact it was tortuous to me. I would work 60 hours a week at least and it was mostly crunching numbers with very little interpersonal interaction. I am somewhat of a social butterfly, so the desk work was driving me crazy.

You might ask then why I chose this course of study and career path. Truth be told, I had no mentor or direction in High School. I was under the assumption that a person had two paths to choose from. You can go the science route or the math route. Since I was mathematically inclined I chose accounting. I knew I would get a job, and I guess the security was important to me at the time.

In New York City, there were many recruiting firms that specialized in taking young people with two years experience from the "Big 8" firms and placing them in various banking and brokerage companies in the city. I happened to get a call one day from one of those recruiters. The timing was perfect as I had just decided that I was not only done with public accounting, but accounting in general. I told the recruiter this over the phone and he convinced me to come and speak to him in person. In the middle of the interview, he asked if I would consider working for him in recruiting. I was so fed up with what I was doing that I said emphatically, "Yes!"

I became very successful in recruiting, as my outgoing, aggressive personality took over and I was doing really well. The firm was called A/L Associates, and they were one of the larger recruiting firms in New York City. They had an accounting division, a banking division, a secretarial division, a legal division, a computer division, as well as a prestigious investment banking division. I progressed very quickly to Vice President in just three years time.

I was doing very well financially at the young age of 26. After a three year period at A/L Associates, a co-worker of mine and I decided to open our very own recruiting firm. So, in 1986, Batten Management was born. We acquired many accounts like Banker's Trust, Bear Stearns, Dean Witter, and Morgan Stanley. We also hired three other recruiters in no time and were humming along.

I was listed as the President of the company. So now I said, "Well, Dad, I did it! I have become a Jewish president!"

## SOMETHING IS MISSING

By 1984, I began to make a very comfortable income. I had a luxury condominium, as well as two other rental luxury apartments. I had an expensive sports car, investments, and much money in the bank. I was no John Paul Getty, but for a poor schnook from the Bronx, who grew up in a low income housing project, I was doing well and I felt I was making my de-

Me on a trip to California

ceased father proud. (He had died with only $100 cash to his name.) However, with all my success, there was still something missing. I wasn't sure what that something was, but you know the drill, if you ask, you get answers; if you seek, you just may find; and if you knock, a door may open for you. So where does a nice, Jewish boy go for answers? Anywhere but God!

I got involved in Eastern philosophy which involved looking for answers by reaching a higher level of consciousness. What I got was pride, arrogance, and a lot of confusion. It was 1985 and I was very involved in martial arts—Karate, Kung Fu, Tae Kwon Do, etc. I stumbled on a special school with a teacher that was beyond excellence in terms of martial arts ability and in teaching those skills. I had to be extensively interviewed to get in as this was no ordinary martial arts academy. In fact, there was no fee for the teaching. We were just required to have devotion to the art and its philosophy. We would physically train for hours on end and spend an equal, if not greater, amount of time on spiritual training in Eastern thought and religions. To put it bluntly, this was more of a cult than a martial arts school, with underpinnings of the occult. We read from the Baghaveda, the I Ching, and became immersed in transcendental meditation. I actually sat in meditation for three hours once.

I was the teacher's top student, with all the other students wishing they were me. I was climbing the ladder to becoming somewhat of my own little god. (I am embarrassed to write this, but it is true and I want to be perfectly honest.)

## MEETING BERNADETTE

Life was great. I was a world traveler. I had money to spend and a whole lot of confidence. I was also a work-out maniac, and I worshipped my body. So, one night I decided to go to Jack Lalanne's in Yonkers. I had a friend who was their regional manager so he let me work-out there whenever I wanted. I walked in that evening, and there was this striking beauty behind the desk. She was absolutely stunning with long black hair, gorgeous blue eyes, and a 10 physique. I was talking to my friend who also happened to be at the desk. He asked if I wanted to use his condominium in Florida. I replied, "I would love to but I have no one to go with."

Then this lovely, young lady perked up and said, "How long do I have to pack a bag?"

I thought to myself, *Wow! Looks and a sense of humor! This is too good to be true!* I asked her out that night. Appropriately enough it was in February right before Valentine's Day. The rest is history.

When we met, I was 25 and she was 18. In many ways, though, she was more mature than I. She had already been living on her own and supporting herself since the tender age of 16. Needless to say, she was very independent. The youngest of six children, she grew up in the Bronx, not in a housing project but a small apartment building on the west side of the Bronx near Van Cortlandt Park. She was raised Roman Catholic in an Irish neighborhood. She attended twelve years of Catholic school but never went to college.

Her father died when she was a young teen. Her mother met another man who had a small house upstate. He and her mom wanted to move up there. Bernadette was the only child still living at home at the time. Her mom begged her to move with them, but she refused. Instead she stayed in the Bronx with her sister and pursued a career in acting and modeling while working as a personal trainer in New York City, which is how I met her.

On our second date when I drove to pick her up, her neighborhood seemed so bad to me that I didn't want to get out of the car. She had moved in with a divorced girl who had three kids. I had a $2000 monthly spending account at the time and made over a hundred grand a year. I had sort of a "savior" complex. So I said to her, "I don't know if we will keep on dating or not, but I can't let you live where you are living. I've got to get you out of here." Needless to say, my concern and ability to help impressed her.

We fell in love, but our relationship was quite rocky because I was a selfish man. I really had no desire to be married as I just did not see the benefit. But I do remember saying to a friend of mine that if I was to ever get married, Bernadette would be the one.

# SEARCHING FOR TRUTH

In 1986 my Martial Arts teacher began speaking about the Bible and Jesus Christ which I thought was downright weird. I mean I could see how Eastern thought could relate to martial arts, but the Bible? Being of Jewish heritage, I could listen to almost any and all teaching relating to New Age thinking, but when he started talking about Jesus, I had to check out. I was taught as a young man, that we, as Jewish people, had nothing to do with Jesus. I knew nothing about Him except that He was the leader of the Catholic Church, and we were Jewish. In other words, you can't dance at two weddings.

So I began to pull away from the school. I remember feeling deeply wounded and very insecure when I left. I felt as though I was leaving my lifeline, which is the way most cults are designed to make you feel.

However, I missed the training so much and this particular teacher possessed such a tremendous charisma that had such an incredible hold on me that I decided it would be okay to delve a bit in the Bible, and in a short time I returned back to the school. (Bernadette was also attending. She loved the teacher. She had not been a practicing Catholic since she graduated from Catholic high school.) Although they were preaching the Bible, there were still some eastern philosophical undertones, like their belief in reincarnation etc. It was quite an involved group. We studied every Tuesday night. The meeting would start at 6 pm and last until midnight or 1:00 am.

While reading the New Testament for these study nights, I came across a story that appeared to be quite spectacular, and it occurred at a place called the "Transfiguration Mount". Interestingly enough, I had an internal desire to go there. I'm not sure why, I just did. It was there that Yeshua (Jesus) showed up along with two very dead guys, Moses and Elijah. It seemed like an incredible event to me, not just because two pillars of my faith who had been certifiably dead for a very long time showed up, but I wondered, "What in the world were they doing with Jesus?"

At any rate I continued to read the Bible without having any real understanding of it. I was also developing my very own religion, mixing some aspects of Buddhism, Hinduism, and Taoism with some Biblical principles.

A couple of years later when I was reading more of the New Testament, there was this one group of verses that when I read them, I began to cry inconsolably. It was in the fourteenth chapter of the Gospel according to John! In the first three verses of the New International Version, it states, *"Do not let your hearts be troubled. Trust in God; trust also in me. In my Father's house are many rooms; if it were not so, I would have told you. I am going there to prepare a place for you. And if I go and prepare a place for you, I will come back and take you to be with me that you also may be where I am."* Now I can't explain to you just what I experienced the very first time I read those words, but I remember it like it was yesterday. I was sitting on my couch in my living room in my apartment in New York. I remember crying and crying as I read those few lines of Scripture. All I can say is that when I read those words, somehow I was utterly convinced that this guy could not lie.

All my life I was on a secret quest to find the truth. For that matter, I believe we all are. I was looking for something or someone who would tell me the truth no matter what. I searched and searched the world over, but I always came up short. I became frustrated when I realized that if I, myself, can't be honest with me, then who in the world could be? I came to the conclusion that all men are liars—of course, some more than others. Some maliciously, as opposed to non-maliciously, but nevertheless, all men lie! When I read those three lines in John 14, somehow, someway I really wanted to believe them.

Long story short, the Lord was working on me, and this was only the beginning. Although I was looking for love in all the wrong places, as the song goes, I was in fact looking for love. The Lord is so gracious, so merciful, so loving, so tender, so patient, and so good, that He would begin to help navigate me to the Truth, which was Himself!

In the midst of all my seeking, somehow my mind was changed about marriage. Suddenly, I wanted to get married. So, one night, I proposed to Bernadette at my apartment over a nice romantic dinner I had prepared.

For our wedding, we couldn't put my mom in a Catholic Church nor Bernadette's mom in a synagogue. So I rented the Tarrytown House in Tarrytown, New York. It is a gorgeous old castle on the scenic Hudson River. Our guest list consisted of only 100 people with 18 of those guests being in the wedding party. We wanted to invite only those who really wanted to be there and genuinely celebrate with us. The Officiant who married us was a colleague of mine who worked for another executive search firm. She and I had done a little work together. (Our firms sometimes helped each other out in recruiting, the way real estate agencies help each other out in selling houses.) When she found out about our wedding predicament, she said, "I'm a justice of peace. Why don't you let me preside over your wedding?" We were pleased to have her. The interesting thing is that her father was a Rabbi in New York City! It was a beautiful wedding ceremony on a circular slate patio overlooking the Hudson River. The weather was perfect in spite of just following Hurricane Hugo that hit South Carolina. The strong winds and torrential rains from Hugo were still hitting New York the night before our scheduled nuptials. Miraculously, God provided a perfect day for our event.

I thank God He brought Bernadette and I together. It is obvious to me that it was meant to be, but the enemy would try again and again to destroy it.

Now, before we get to the honeymoon, I want to tell you a funny story that happened later on in my life. I was staying temporarily at a friend of a friend's house on a lake near Macon, Georgia. We were moving there from Florida. I soon discovered that this house was somewhat of a home for the fishing enthusiast. Growing up in New York City, fishing was something I heard about but had never done! I came to the realization that fishing was a part of the culture in Georgia, so I may as well give it a try.

47

There was a plethora of rods in the house, so I grabbed one and went to purchase some worms at the local worm store. Some call it a bait shop, I believe. I strolled out on the dock adjacent to the house and cast my hook in the water.

I thought to myself, *How hard could this possibly be?* Each day I attempted to hook a fish, but I came up empty. I think I got the reputation in the lake as the guy who feeds the fish as opposed to the guy who catches them! I felt as if every time I strolled out on the dock the fish began laughing and said to each other, "Hey guys, here comes the New York Jew. It's feeding time!"

It was the last week that I was going to reside at the lake. I wanted to catch a fish so badly that I actually prayed, "Oh Lord, please let me catch a fish, just one." Well, the incredible happened. Lo and behold a fish was caught! I gave out a scream, "I got one! I really got one!" I felt as if it was a miraculous catch. The Lord had answered my prayer!

As I attempted to get the fish off the hook, I cut my hand! Unbeknownst to me it was a catfish! One of the smallest catfish on record, I may add. I went into the house, grabbed a dish towel, came back and performed the task at hand of getting the fish off the hook. To my surprise, the fish came off the hook nicely, but it became one with the dishtowel. As much as I don't want to admit it, I began to beat the dishtowel on the dock, in hopes that I would separate the fish from the towel.

At this point I noticed a little fishing boat approaching me carrying an elderly chap with a long beard, dressed in a white tee shirt and a pair of well-worn overalls. To my surprise, he pulled right up to the dock and asked the following question, "Where you from?"

To which I answered, "Macon."

"No, where you from?"

"Well, actually, I just moved here from Florida."

He then more emphatically repeated the question a third time, "Where you from?"

"Originally New York City."

"Right."

I pictured this man going to the local watering hole that night and saying to his friends, "You ain't gonna believe this!"

Well, I am about to tell you a story about how my wife and I were arrested and captivated by God's love, grace, and mercy, and all I can say is, "You ain't gonna believe this!"

I have experienced the Lord's amazing grace and His tender loving mercies on numerous occasions. I am well aware of the Lord's forgetfulness when it comes to our sins, however, as He says in Isaiah 42:8 (CJB), *"I am ADONAI; that is my name. I yield my glory to no one else, nor my praise to any idol."*

With that being said, let me pray.

*Father, I pray that this testimonial to Your love and power brings You great pleasure. I pray, Father God, that many would see and many would hear and You would be lifted higher than You are right now! Father, what is a dead dog like me doing dining at Your table? All I can say is thank You, Abba!*

In this Spirit, let us embark on our journey together.

# CHAPTER THREE

# SEEING THE LIGHT

It was September 25, 1989, and I had been married now for all of twenty four hours! I was with my beautiful bride in a shiny black limousine en route to John F. Kennedy International Airport in New York City to catch an El Al flight to Israel to begin our honeymoon. You may ask why a nonbeliever was going to Israel for a honeymoon, as I myself was asking the same question.

Many Jewish people can be indifferent towards Israel, especially those residing in the States. I, myself, knew very little about the Holy Land. I knew a little of Israel's history from my days in Hebrew school, but we were far removed from the goings on in the land. I had absolutely no desire to go and visit Israel, especially for a honeymoon. I never felt as though the place was safe, or a place of beauty. Boy, did my opinion ever change once I toured the land of milk and honey!

I was financially successful from the mid to late eighties. During that time I traveled extensively all throughout the Caribbean. I loved the islands and the white sandy beaches. The cool, tropical evening breezes were to die for. Being so in love with the Caribbean, it was only natural that we honeymoon there at some tropical island resort where we could dine on exotic foods, swim in the pristine waters, sunbathe along magnificent beaches, and get massages while the beautiful breezes gently caress our skin.

How in the world did this dream turn into a trip to Israel? Well, one day, a man that I had become very close with and whom I respected immensely, told me I should go to Israel to honeymoon. I thought to myself, *You must be crazy.* The next day, I was on the train going into the city and I sat next to a man who happened to be Jewish. He told me that if I ever wanted to visit Israel, he worked for El Al airlines and his father-in-law was well connected with Israel. He could put together a wonderful itinerary for me.

The Bible speaks of the Lord's Spirit working in us and on us prior to actually being transformed, and this was His work. I can't explain why, but I felt my heart was pulled in the direction of Israel even though everything in my head was screaming *Jamaica!* Then again, the Bible says that the Lord holds the hearts of kings in His hands and guides them like streams of water. So if He could guide a prince, He could certainly guide a pauper as well.

It's been said the heart of a Jew is Jerusalem, and I guess I was off to find my heart! I must tell you, just to be on the safe side, I added a week on the tail end of the honeymoon to visit the Greek Isles as well. We left New York City early in the morning and arrived the next day at Ben Gurion Airport in Tel Aviv only to catch another flight to Eilat, where we were to begin our journey. Eilat is located in the southernmost tip of the country. It is a beautiful spot right on the northern tip of the Red Sea, amidst the loveliest landscape, nestled nicely in the Sinai mountain range with Saudi Arabia in its sight. Eilat is somewhat of a resort playground for the Israelis, like the Caribbean was for me. Since I knew all too well how to play, I felt right at home. So far, we were not doing so badly after all.

I think I need to explain again here. You see I was thirty years young and I was doing very well financially. I was the president of a boutique executive search firm, specializing in the disciplines of banking and finance. This was a time when the economy was flourishing and I was flourishing along with it! I spent my summers at the beach, and my winters skiing. You would find me going off to the Caribbean islands every three months for some rest and relaxation, along with a fair amount of good old-fashioned fun! Life was good and life was easy, and I didn't have a care in the world!

So here I was in Eilat on the Red Sea. Here was the place where one of the greatest events in the history of my people, as well as the body of believers for that matter, transpired. The Exodus of the Hebrew children from their oppressors in Egypt occurred in this very locale! Let's face it, no exodus, no Jewish people. No Jewish people, no tribes of Israel. No tribes of Israel, no tribe of Judah. No tribe of Judah, no Lion of Judah. No Lion of Judah, heaven forbid! I think you get the picture.

At any rate, here I was in Eilat along the Red Sea. The very spot where the Lord miraculously parted the waters so the Hebrew people were able to walk across on dry land. Then the Lord in His infinite wisdom, mercy and power connected the waters once again so the Egyptian army would be consumed and overcome! Well, I'm sure most people of faith would have been overwhelmed and altogether exhilarated to be in such an incredible place, but I had other plans. I would be spending time on the Red Sea alright, but I would be scuba diving under the sea and water skiing on top of it! I would go out for gourmet dinners followed up by some late night dancing! We even went on a camel ride in the Sinai Desert one day and got a beautiful view of four countries.

After a few days of fun and frolic, it was time to continue our journey in Israel by heading north to Jerusalem. So we hopped a flight and off we went to Jerusalem for a few days. We decided to visit the Old City as it is chock full of historic sights and sounds and is a must see as far as world travelers are concerned. Believe it or not Jerusalem is considered one of the most international cities in the world with folks coming from all the nations. However, I must be honest with you, once we arrived in Jerusalem, I was already missing Eilat.

It almost sounds comical to me as I write the "Old" City. In the United States, if we find a structure a couple of hundred years old, we consider it old. As I traveled around parts of Europe, I found structures from the 1400's. We Americans consider them really old. But in Israel, you have structures dated 1400 B.C!

As we were strolling around the Old City, to my dismay, I became confused and a tad despondent. Please excuse my presumptuous nature, but I just assumed in Jerusalem you'd find predominantly Jewish people. Never did I expect to see so many mosques and churches in what I assumed was a "Jewish" city.

Israel is all of 7,900 square miles in the middle of eight million square miles of Arab territory. Allow me to illustrate this vast contrast. Let us use a typical football field and say this is representative of the Arab territory. Then place a common book of matches on the fifty yard line. If the football field is the Arab lands, then the book of matches is the land mass known as Israel. The land of Israel is less than the size of the small state of New Jersey. In fact, it is the size of metro Atlanta! Why would someone who owns eight million square miles be interested in just a piddly, little land of 7,900 square miles that has no oil?   If only Moses hadn't obeyed the Lord at the time of the Exodus. If only instead of making a left turn after leaving Egypt, he went straight; then the Jews would have owned Saudi Arabia, and I would be spending about 40 cents per gallon for gasoline! But obedience is better than sacrifice, and Moses was the servant of the Lord.

It's amazing to me that the Lord was able to carve out a piece of land without any oil, in the midst of so much oil embedded territory. I think maybe the Lord wants His children to depend on Him as their supernatural resource and not on natural resources.

At any rate, while surveying the Old City of Jerusalem, I found a Jewish quarter, a Christian quarter, an Armenian quarter, and a Muslim quarter. I thought to myself, *Why in the world is Jerusalem so divided? Capital cities of other countries are not divided this way, only Israel's.* I have traveled to Germany, Ireland, England, Wales, India, Kenya, etc. What I found in Ireland was the Irish, in Wales the Welsh, in Germany, Germans, etc. etc. I don't want to sound exclusive, divisional, or arrogant, but I bet you will find Spaniards in

Spain!! I later found out when I read the whole Bible, that the land is God's land and for whatever reason, He gave title and deed to the children of Israel forever, and who are we to argue with the Creator and Sustainer of the universe?

After a couple days of touring Jerusalem, I just became more and more uncomfortable there. Little did I know that Jerusalem is the city with more spiritual warfare hovering over it than any other city in the world. Israel is the most spiritually attacked country as well. You see, the devil and the Lord are in a battle for who will control the Temple Mount and who will rule and reign over the world! I'm no betting man, but if I was, I would bet the Lord is going to win! It's not about the land, but the Lord and the city of the Great King.

Since we were feeling uncomfortable in the Old City, I mentioned to my wife that maybe we should consider going to the Sea of Galilee in the morning. Galilee is due north of Jerusalem. We only had two days left in Israel, and the second day would have to be a travel day as we would then be off on the last leg of our trip—the beautiful Greek Isles. If we were going to travel to the northern region of Israel, we had but one chance, and only one day to do it!

The next morning, we went to a car rental office and to our surprise they were closed because of the High Holidays, Rosh Hashanah and Yom Kippur. Yes, I was that far removed from my Jewish roots that I was unaware we were right smack in the middle of the Holiest days on the Jewish calendar. You see, after I paid my penance to Judaism and had my Bar Mitzvah, I decided to begin my journey away from the synagogue and the Jewish lifestyle.

Interestingly enough, one of the employees at the car rental office happened to be there catching up on some paper work and we managed to get noticed. Although there are many devout Jews in the land of Israel, there are many secular humanists as well. When this one particular employee heard my last name, "Hershberg", she realized I was Jewish;

and because I was not in Temple, she probably assumed I was secular as well. She showed us favor and we got a car. I thought to myself, *This is the very first time it paid to have a last name with "-berg" on the end of it.*

As I mentioned earlier, I had experienced a fair amount of anti-Semitism growing up in the Bronx. I was familiar with the Holocaust and other Jewish persecutions, and I was one of those Jews who thought, *Lord if we are the "chosen" people, then maybe You should choose someone else?* I don't mean to be disrespectful to the Lord, I just want to be transparent and share with you what I believe are the sentiments of many of my people.

After completing the paperwork, we got in our rental car and off we were to Galilee. I was hoping to find the Mount of Transfiguration that I had read about in the New Testament. I thought that it would be neat to stand on the same mountain where the incredible "transfiguration" event with Moses and Elijah took place, even if I did not necessarily believe it myself! We really did not know where to go as we had no plan. But since the country is the size of New Jersey, I thought we would find our way eventually.

In 1989, many of the Israeli soldiers would hitchhike to get around. Because my wife and I are very friendly and quite social and were not intimidated being raised in the inner city of New York, we stopped along the way and gave these brave men and women rides. I thought it was somewhat of an insurance marker to have a passenger who just happened to have a loaded gun in our car. It was like having our very own personal bodyguard.

When we arrived at Galilee, we noticed yet another soldier hitchhiking. So naturally, we pulled the car over and rolled down the window and asked if he spoke English, to which he responded, "Of course." Although Hebrew is the national tongue in Israel, English is very prevalent as well. It is taught as a second language in school. I asked if he knew where the Transfiguration Mount was. He didn't.

He then asked me if we would give him a ride to Tabor. He gave us directions and off to Tabor we drove. We drove a short distance and he told us to pull the vehicle over. We obliged, of course. As I said, he had a loaded gun. He was very appreciative and we said our good-byes.

To my surprise, on my left was a huge, beautiful mountain that gave me a strange feeling. I don't know how else to describe the sensation, except to say that the mountain was calling my name. I felt as though it wasn't only calling my name, but it was tugging at me. My heart felt as if it was going to jump out of my chest. I felt as though a giant hook came from off the top of the mountain, dug into my chest and was reeling me in.

I started to drive up the mountain pretty aggressively. If you are familiar with New York City drivers, you will understand what I mean. I drove faster and faster up this very treacherous course with no guard rails and no pavement. I had to get to the top and I had to get there fast! Why you ask? I don't know, except to say not only did I feel compelled to get to the top of this mountain, but I felt somewhat possessed, like I wasn't driving the car but the car was driving me! I felt as though I was on a mission, yet I did not know why. I remember it like it was yesterday. I know I was going dangerously fast, as I can still hear Bernadette screaming all the way up!

When we finally reached the summit, I literally swung the door open and jumped from the car. Bernadette followed quickly behind me. She was very relieved to set her feet on solid ground. There was a huge fence ahead. I ran to the only entrance gate I could see at the top of the mountain and proceeded to go inside. As I marched further in, I saw a basilica and noticed a plaque on the wall. When I got close to the plaque I was able to read the inscription which stated, "The Basilica to the Transfiguration." I couldn't believe it! I was on the very mountain to which I felt a desperate need to find!

Little did I know Mount Tabor and the Transfiguration Mount were one and the same! The actual name of the mountain is Tabor, however, some Biblical students call it "The Transfiguration Mount" in honor of the event that took place there!

My knees started to buckle and I got very woozy. I heard a voice say, "Come away with Me and pray." I wanted to do as the voice directed me, but I was at a loss. I am embarrassed to say that I did not know how to pray, nor did I know the components of prayer. As I mentioned, I had spent a considerable amount of time with some Eastern religious philosophies and their arts of meditation, as well as some other "cult" practices. All I knew to do was to find a quiet place to be alone and empty out my mind. I walked into a garden area which was quite secluded and found a three tiered rock to climb up on. I was on the tallest part of the Mount and, although there were some other people at the site, I felt very much alone. I closed my eyes and attempted to empty my thoughts.

With my eyes closed and my thoughts as empty as they could possibly be, I began to see a vision. It was almost like a movie playing in my head. I saw the eastern sky open like a veil being torn from top to bottom! I saw a figure of a man come from behind the veil as it was being ripped from the heavenlies. His face shown like the sun, and His clothes were white as light. He floated down from the sky and pressed Himself upon me, chest to chest, face to face. He looked like a typical Israeli with dark eyes, dark hair, and dark skin. Go figure!

He began to speak directly into my ear. He told me first and foremost, that He loved me. He told me that He was the one I was reading about in the Old Testament. (As some say, the Old Testament is the New Testament concealed, and the New Testament is the Old Testament revealed.) He then told me that He was going to build a place for me and He would come back for me, all I had to do was believe that He is the

Messiah. This made me recall those verses that had made me cry a year or so earlier.

When the Lord spoke to me on the top of that mountain it was as if all I was ever looking for was found in HIM! For some reason I believed Him. Could I have been saved? This was a conspiracy of God's grace for sure! Hey, I was just honeymooning, right? I was just touring the northern countryside, minding my own business.

I love when people say they found the Lord, like it was He who was lost. No way, my friends. The Lord finds us each and every time. I began to cry. No, sob. No, weep. Yes, weep! I couldn't stop weeping no matter how hard I tried. I thought to myself, *Why am I crying so much and why can't I stop?*

Looking back on it, I would have to say it was definitely not a cry of pain nor was it a cry of joy exactly. I believe it was a sanctifying cry. The Lord was cleansing me from the inside out—beginning the process of emptying me of me and filling me with Him!

Bernadette, who had been investigating the site nearby, came and asked, "What's wrong? Why are you crying?"

"I've just met God," I told her between sobs. She didn't say anything then, but she said later that she felt a little confused. She wondered, *How did I miss this God encounter? I was RIGHT HERE!!* She kept whining to the Lord about this the rest of the visit.

Well, I cried off and on for about twenty minutes on the top of that mountain. Finally, I heard Bernadette say, "Greg, we have to go, or we won't have time to see the other sites in the area. We have to get back to Jerusalem by nightfall to pack up our belongings and head out to Greece in the morning!"

Bernadette and I had what I would call a very secular relationship for some time. Let's just say it was not all that spiritual, and definitely not God-centered. We dated for five years prior to getting married and although we were very fond of each other, a cord of two has little hope, if any, of survival, especially these days! I told my new wife, "I don't want to leave this mountain."

"What?!" She was a bit irritated at that response, being anxious to move on.

"I do not want to leave."

She then said sarcastically (sarcasm being part of our New York fabric, mind you), "So you're going to stay on this mountain forever, are you?"

To which I responded with a resounding, "Yes!"

You see, I had experienced many exhilarating moments in my life and let me highlight the word moments as they were fleeting at best and always needing refueling with no lasting effects. I never, ever felt the way I felt at that moment on top of that mountain. I felt as if whatever was missing in my life was now in place. The last piece of the puzzle took up residence in my heart and I was complete, or should I say completed with nothing lacking.

Even though I had a "full life" at thirty years young, having experienced much in my quest for peace and purpose, it was as if I had been an orphan my whole entire life and had now finally met my Father.

But to my surprise my Father had been looking for me all along. His desire was that we would be together forever, because He wanted me. He even craved for me so much that He had been on a search and rescue mission for my soul all along. I now realized that He was miserable without me and I was truly miserable without Him. I realized that I would never, ever be alone again. He would always be there for me no matter what. The search was over and I would never again be found looking for love. It was as if there was a God-shaped hole in my heart that had finally been filled.

You may ask why I couldn't leave the mountain. Well, Peter, James and John who were there some 2,000 years before me didn't want to leave that mountain either!

You see, I had no conception of the indwelling of God's Spirit. I did not know that we were, in fact, temples of God's

Holy Spirit. I was under the impression that if I left the mountain, I would leave His presence, and if I left His presence I would be right back where I started. So I figured because I had never, ever felt this good before, if I left I would never, ever feel like this again. I wanted to just camp out on the mountain! Foolish maybe, but hopefully you can understand not wanting to lose that loving feeling. Sounds like a sparkling deduction if you ask me. Just remain here and you remain in His love. However, I finally came to my senses, or shall I say I came to grips with the fact that I probably should finish my honeymoon, get back to New York City, and continue on with my life.

Before we left, I told Bernadette I wanted to be alone for a little longer, so she reluctantly gave me some more privacy.

I spoke to the Lord and told Him just how sorry I was that I had to leave. I thanked Him from the very depths of my heart for showing Himself to me. I told Him that although I knew no one would probably ever believe me and I could never prove the vision, it was as real as anything and no one would be able to take it from me. I promised Him that I would come back soon.

I also needed to desperately ask Him a question—a very, very important question at that. You see, as I said, I was raised in an Orthodox synagogue and although my family didn't practice strict Orthodox Judaism, we went to synagogue every Shabbat and I went to Hebrew School two times a week. I was dedicated to the Lord at birth, given my Hebrew name, circumcised on the eighth day, and Bar Mitzvahed in the temple at age thirteen. Until my father died when I was fifteen I sort of tried to live according to the tenets of the faith. By the way, just on a side note, I failed miserably. I did not know God well because intimacy with the Lord was something we never discussed in Hebrew School, but I knew of Him through our external religious practices. Today, when I read about Abraham, Isaac, and Jacob, Moses, Joshua, etc.,

I see people who had wonderfully intimate relationships with the Lord. I don't know where all this intimacy went to in Judaism, but maybe too much external religious ritual can snuff out internal, relational reality.

In any event, Judaism is kind of interesting in that although it is one of the three major religions of the world, Christianity and Islam being the other two, it is also a nationality of sorts! Due to the incredible minority (the Jewish people represent less than 1/5 of 1% of the world's population), coupled with the incredible amount of persecution we have had to endure just for having last names like Hershberg, we see Judaism as not only a bona-fide religion, but more importantly as a nationality. So when I was young and I was asked what nationality I was, I would say unswervingly, "I am Jewish!" My other friends would say Italian, or Spanish, or Irish, etc., but I would always say, "I'm Jewish!"

Growing up in New York City, I was under the impression that you could fall into one of three religious categories which were as follows: Jewish, Catholic, or Atheist! By the way, even if a Jew is not practicing his or her religion, they cannot deny they are Jewish. It's like the 614th commandment. Thou shalt not give Hitler the victory!

So, although I had not been practicing my Jewish faith since I was Bar Mitzvah-ed, I was still 100% Jewish! So before I left the mountain, I desperately needed to clarify something in my own mind. I could not leave until I was clear on a very important issue. Here is the question I posed to the Lord.

"Now that I believe that You, Yeshua (Jesus) are the prophesied Messiah as stated by the prophets of old in the Old Testament, I guess I have to stop being Jewish and give up Judaism, right?"

I heard the answer from His voice as clear as day, "Why? I didn't!"

"What do You mean, You didn't?" I questioned in my mind. "You are the head of the Catholic church. You started a "new" religion, didn't You?"

64

I didn't know Yeshua was Jewish, and I thought for sure I must be the only Jewish person in the universe that believes in Him, so now what do I do? What do I call myself, and where do I go from here? As a young man, there was absolutely no mention of Yeshua (Jesus) in my synagogue, in my household, among my Gentile friends, or in my life at all. We had nothing against Him per se; we just had nothing to do with Him. Or shall I say He had nothing to do with us, or so I thought.

I meditated on His answer a bit but I had no idea what He meant when He said, "I didn't give up being Jewish." So off I went with my bride down the mountain holding on to my question and answer session loosely. By the time we got to the bottom of that mountain, the answer meant very little to me.

Little did I know that the answer to that question would later become the focal point of my ministry to bring the lost sheep of the house of Israel and the "Church of Jesus Christ" into agreement through the Messiah Himself—Jew and Gentile, one in Messiah. The Jewish people need to know that Yeshua is King of the Jews, their King! They need to know that they don't have to stop being Jewish because Judaism is not the problem. Sadly enough, Judaism is not necessarily the answer either! Sin is the problem and Yeshua is the answer!

By the same token, the Christian community must come to the realization according to the Bible, especially the 11th chapter in the letter written to the Romans (Gentile believers), that Jesus is Jewish, and that they are, in fact, grafted into the olive tree. Shaul (Saul), a.k.a. the great Apostle Paul, tells us in Romans 11:18 that the Gentile people don't support the root, but the root supports them. The middle wall of partition has been torn down by the blood of Messiah and now we are one, Jew and Gentile in Messiah Yeshua! We shall look further into this very important matter later as it has caused much confusion over the years for the believing community at large. But for now we have to get down off the mountain and continue on our journey.

I was literally leaving my mountaintop experience, and we were on our way to see one more sight! We had decided to go and see Capernaum, but before we go off to Capernaum, let me make a very important statement to those who have not come to the realization that Yeshua is, in fact, the prophesied Messiah, for this is the very heart of the matter. (See John 5:45-46.) In the prophetic writings of the Bible, like Isaiah, Jeremiah, Ezekiel, etc., they speak of the Jewish people being scattered about the world (which is known as the Diaspora). They would, in fact, be in exile for many years, but the Lord in His infinite grace, mercy, and love would supernaturally return those scattered Jewish people from the very four corners of the world and return them physically to the nation of Israel. Once they return physically back to the land, the Lord would miraculously return them spiritually back to Himself, via somewhat of a spiritual heart transplant. This is discussed succinctly in Jeremiah 31:31-34, saying it is done through a "New Covenant", returning us spiritually back to God through the atoning death of Messiah.

Truth be told, right now as we speak, I am a fulfillment of God's prophetic word and a living, breathing testimony of His faithfulness. I am a Jew who was living in the Diaspora, not in the land of Israel. According to Scripture, at some point I must return. Look at the 36th chapter of Ezekiel in the 24th verse (CJB), *"For I will take you [the Jewish people to which I belong, of course] from among the nations, gather you* [the Jewish People] *from all the countries,* [the United States being one of those countries, of course] *and return you* [the Jewish People] *to your own soil* [the Land of Israel]." Continuing on, God declares, *"Then I will sprinkle clean water on you, and you will be clean; I will cleanse you from all your uncleanness and from your idols. I will give you a new heart* [born anew] *and put a new spirit inside you* [the Ruach, the Holy Spirit]; *I will take the stony heart out of your flesh and give you a heart of flesh; I will put my Spirit inside you and cause you to live by my laws, respect my rulings and obey them."*

Now, I purposely didn't want to use an over abundance of Scripture in this book, as I really want to reach out to those who may not see the Bible as authentically God-breathed. I can tell you though, having read many holy books from the Baghavedas to the I Ching, as well as parts of the Koran, I finally decided that all these sacred writings could not possibly all be right. Truth had to be absolute! I proceeded to test all of them. The Bible won, hands down. Let me explain.

I have spent a great deal of time studying the Bible's authenticity. In doing so I even studied C. Sanders' book, *Introduction In Research In English Literary History*. C. Sanders is a military expert and historian as well as the top expert in the world in authenticating literary documents. He penned in his book that there are three tests for the reliability of a literary document. (1) Bibliographical evidence, which is the textural tradition from the original document to the copies and manuscripts we possess today, as well as the number of copies and the time span from the original events; (2) The internal evidence, which is what the document actually says and claims itself as well as whether each and every apparent discrepancy can be reconciled; and (3) The external evidence, which is how the document aligns itself with facts, dates, and persons in historical events recorded outside the document itself. In Mr. Sanders' expert study, the Bible passes all three of these tests of authenticity amazingly well.

Robert Laird Harris (March 10, 1911 – April 25, 2008), a Presbyterian minister and Old Testament scholar, said in his work, *Can I Trust My Bible?*, "We can now be sure that copyists worked with great care and accuracy on the Old Testament even back to 225 B.C. and indeed it would be rash skepticism that would now deny that we have our Old Testament in a form very close to that used by Ezra when he taught the Word of the Lord to those who had returned from the Babylonian captivity."

Now, if this is true, which I wholeheartedly contend that it is true, then what the prophets prophesied must come to pass, otherwise it would be a false prophesy and we would be pitied most among men! When Ezekiel spoke that the Jewish people would return from the four corners of the world and come back to Israel, we had a problem. You see not only were the children of Israel scattered, but the very land itself was in other hands out of the control of the Jewish people. So the problem was twofold. One, can the people just fly on the wings of eagles so to speak? Secondly, how can they return to a land that they don't possess? There are two words that I just love saying together, "But God."

But God, in 1948, miraculously, to say the least, birthed the nation of Israel in one day—just like Isaiah said in Isaiah 66:8! Then in 1967, supernaturally, Jerusalem was back in the hands of the Jewish people for the first time since the year 70—as the prophet Daniel prophesied in the book of Daniel chapter 9, some 2500 years before the event took place! Although it seemed like the Lord was slow with His promises, He is never ever late and His timing is perfect.

Ezekiel also makes reference to the fact that not only would the Jewish people return to the land physically, but spiritually as well and receive what the Prophet calls the "new heart" as I pointed out earlier. We are referring to a "new" heart figuratively as opposed to literally.

My point is this, did I not, a Jewish man, return to the land supernaturally in 1989? Did I not receive the "new heart" as well? I mean how in the world do you explain me leaving New York as a very self-centered, financially successful entrepreneur, without a desire to serve God whatsoever, and returning 100% changed, ready to quit my job and say goodbye to everything I held near and dear, to pursue the Lord and the things of His Kingdom? Exactly! That's why I say, it's supernatural and altogether hard to explain, as most Spirit things tend to be.

Well, let me tell you, I have not looked back! Not one day! I have been walking hard with the Lord now for over twenty years. And the good news is, you could have this awesome experience as well.

You may say that you cannot be all that God wants you to be because you have so many issues that need to be dealt with, or you've done things that you yourself can't forgive, so how can God? The fact is, I had so many issues as well and still have a few twenty years later, but if I could work out all the issues myself then I wouldn't need God in the first place.

The initial step is to turn around from where you are and turn to God. Tell Him you want to change, but you just can't on your own. Be honest and real with the Lord. If He really is God, then obviously He is omniscient, which is a fancy word that means He knows what's going on anyway. So I would just get real with Him and tell Him that you need Him to change you. Ask Him if He would be willing to take you in and change you.

I have one last very important thing to share. Just as you would not go to someone's house to dine without bringing a gift, or go to a party empty handed, neither should you come to a King, especially the King of all Kings, empty handed. There is no greater gift you could bring than the one God provided for you. In other words, if you bring a gift on your own then you would get the credit as the gift-giver and His gift would lose its value. Bottom line, the Lord wants to receive full credit for this gift so you will know just how much you are worth to Him and that you are loved. Also, you must understand that love is sacrifice, and the greater the sacrifice, the greater the love. The gift is the blood of His very own and very unique Son, Yeshua (Jesus), and there is absolutely no greater sacrifice. So, unless you can come up with a more valuable gift to bring, I would suggest we lay our pride on the shelf and bring Him what is necessary and appropriate, the blood of His Son, Yeshua!

# CHAPTER FOUR

# DISCOVERING
# LIFE

Continuing our honeymoon in the
Old City of Jerusalem in Israel

As I said earlier, we had a chance to see one more site in Galilee as it was getting late in the afternoon. Someone recommended Capernaum, which is actually Kafar Nachum in the original Hebrew language. Kafar Nachum translates into English as *village of comfort*! How appropriate for the Comforter of Israel, Yeshua Himself, to live, minister, and work in the village of comfort! It's like the Bread of Life being born in Bethlehem which translates from Hebrew as *the house of bread*. Capernaum is an amazing site. There are many sites in Israel that we are not totally sure of their exact locale, like the Mount of Beatitudes or the place where Peter was restored on the shores of the Galilee. However, Capernaum is a different story. We are absolutely and unequivocally positive about its coordinates!

When we arrived at the town, we found out it was gated and was operated by the Franciscan monks, a religious order. They have their own rules and regulations that must be adhered to. They denied us entry because, according to their rules, we were not modestly dressed. We were wearing shorts and our knees were exposed. This was a no-no.

You must realize at this point, after meeting the Lord and having an encounter of the divine kind, I believe the Lord was already taking up residence in me. I felt a very strong unction that my wife desperately needed to gain access to the town of Capernaum! I couldn't explain why I felt this way, I just knew we had to get inside. You may relate to the saying, "You just know that you know that you know."

I walked over to the entrance, and spoke to the priest who was the keeper of the gate and asked him if he really believed that the Lord was concerned with our clothing. He did not answer me except to say that it was one of the rules of their order, and there was no way we could enter into the site with the clothes we were wearing. I asked him if the rules of his order abrogated or superseded the rules of God's order. Looking back that was probably not a good idea. As my mother always taught me, "You will catch more bees with honey than you will with vinegar." I then tried to speak to his heart. I told him that we desperately needed to get into the city compound, and we had to leave Israel in the morning and did not know if we would ever be back. When he asked me why we needed to gain access so badly, I really had trouble trying to explain, "All I know is that we need to get inside." Faith smells the fragrance before it sees the flower! Or, as a very famous book states in Hebrews 11:1 (NRSV), "Now faith is the assurance of things hoped for, the conviction of things not seen."

Although we pleaded our case with the gatekeeper, he remained adamant about the dress code. We walked away frustrated, sad, and dejected, realizing that this was our last hoorah in Israel. We would be leaving the next day to go to Greece and who knows when or if we would ever return. As we approached the car dejected in spirit and downright angry in the flesh, the priest who was guarding the gate whistled to us and waved us back. He then held up two pair of workers' pants with a couple of ropes for belts. We ran back over to the gate. We took hold of the clothes, went into the rest room, and threw them on over what we were wearing just as quickly as we could. We were so excited and all I could think was, *Adonai Yireh, the Lord provides!*

We proceeded inside the site to find out that the village was actually quite small. We looked around at some archaeological remains and nothing much caught our fancy until we came upon the remains of a first century synagogue. It actually pulled us in as it was quite stunning in its simplicity.

In the days of the Bible, there was always a local synagogue right smack in the center of the village where the people would come to worship the Lord, learn of His ways, and meet to discuss community issues. It was in the center of the town to symbolize the need for the people to have God in the center of their lives.

We went through what was the apparent entrance to the synagogue. Upon entering, I had this feeling of amazement come over me. I realized that if the Bible account was true, then this is where Yeshua spent much of His young, adult life. If this was the case, then this would also have been the synagogue where he would have taught.

Now I need to mention that except for Shabbat (Sabbath), Yeshua would have spent much more time teaching in the streets, the marketplaces, the highways, and the by-ways. I do not see Yeshua telling His disciples to bring the people to the temple to be saved. He told them to go, and bring the temple to the people! As portrayed earlier, I am in no way, shape, or form a fisherman, but I do have enough sense not to go fishing inside a building. I think the modern day "church" or the body of believers may have it a little backwards.

I tell my people, "You catch 'em and we'll clean 'em." When people ask me where I go to church, my answer usually confuses them. I tell them, "I don't go to church, I am the church. Now if you would like to know where I fellowship, that's a different story altogether." In other words, the Bible tells us if we are born again, then we are the temples of God, filled with His divine Holy Spirit. Therefore, wherever you go, the Light goes with you.

Yeshua, as I mentioned, spent His young, adult life in Capernaum as the Bible states. Since He was a bona-fide, legitimate, Jewish Rabbi, and Capernaum is where He ministered, and since this is the only remains of a synagogue, then we were standing on Holy ground for sure! I was in awe to say the least.

We were standing in the middle of the synagogue which had large stone bench-like seating on the sides like bleachers at a stadium built right into the structure. The synagogues were constructed like that back then so the Word of God could be proclaimed right in the center, as it should be right in the center of our hearts. I had my back to my bride, and being caught up in the emotion of the moment, I blurted out, "Bernadette, can you imagine we are standing on Holy ground? I mean, this is where He taught, and this is where He preached, and this is where we stand. We may be standing on the very ground where He offered up prayers for people and where they were healed. This is the very place where He taught the word of God and raised up talmidim (disciples)."

All of a sudden I heard behind me the sound of knees hitting the ground along with wailing and weeping. I turned around and saw my wife on her face in the synagogue crying her little heart out. I was a tad befuddled at what was going on. I inquired, but she was unresponsive, or shall I say she couldn't respond!

When she finally came around, she told me what had happened. She said she saw a vision of herself with others back 2,000 years ago, sitting in the synagogue. She knew she was back in the first century because in the vision all the people, including her, were dressed in first century traditional garb. She saw Yeshua walking up and down among the people praying for different individuals. When He got to her, He stopped. He placed His blessed hand on her head and said, "Be healed." She said that this meant so much to her as she always wanted to go to medical school and become a doctor but because of circumstances beyond her control, it was not an option. But God in His infinite wisdom and tender mercies sent the Great Physician to her.

Can you believe it? Two encounters in the same day, in the same locale, with not one but two visions—from heaven no less! Never, ever did I think in my wildest imagination that we would leave New York's JFK airport as secular newlyweds far from God and come home eighteen days later a totally different couple. I had no idea that God could do that, nor would I have ever thought that He would do that, but He did. And we have never looked back! As I said, we were looking for love in all the wrong places, but by God's amazing grace, love found us!

Usually you hear of how people came to meet the Lord when they hit rock bottom. It is unusual that you meet the Lord when you are riding high in life and you have the world by a string. Little did I know the world had me, and the string I thought I held onto was in effect choking the life out of me.

# AFTER THE HONEYMOON

Well, the journey got real interesting when we got home. I tend to have an intense, radical personality so I became an intense, radical believer. Like so many others in the Bible who had a God encounter, we were never the same. I personally believe that an encounter with the Lord will change a person forever. Take Paul for instance. He too was radical. He just needed to be re-wired! So I, too, just needed a re-wiring, so to speak, and the Lord would hopefully use all that intensity and obsessiveness for His glory and the furtherance of His kingdom.

After the honeymoon, I quit my job and turned the company over to my partner. We had developed some goodwill in the company, but I was not at all interested in the goodwill, for I had found God's will! I began listening to only faith-based music and I began to tell everyone about the Lord. The enemy doesn't like when Jews come to the fold, because we'll tell everyone. I mean, I was ready to share the Lord with farm animals; I was so zealous and obsessed. I call it O.C.O. - Obsessive Compulsive Order! Yeshua told the Pharisees in Matthew 23:15 that they would go over land and sea to make one proselyte!

I had no mentor, so it was just me and the Lord. I felt compelled to read the Bible. But, as I mentioned before, I struggled horribly with reading comprehension my entire life. I was quite mathematically inclined, but my reading and writing skills were greatly lacking. A friend of mine, whose profession is to diagnose learning disabilities, says I am the classic ADD case, which is an acronym for Attention Deficit Disorder. In fact, he tells me I could be the poster child.

Let me illustrate my struggle in this. The college I attended was renowned for math and accounting. To be accepted, I needed a score of at least 1150 on the SAT exam. Well, there were two sections back then, one was Reading Comprehension and the other was Math, with a maximum score of 800 in each. I scored only 450 in the Reading Comprehension section. But I scored 750 in the Math section which is considered exceptional. This gave me a total score of 1200 which got me into the college!

I hate to admit this, but I had never read an entire book—not even in college—because it was such a daunting task to me. It took so much mental effort for me to understand what I was reading. The Bible was the longest book I had ever seen. It was clearly over the top and out of my grasp. I told the Lord, "Even if I read it, I won't be able to understand it, so what's the use? I love You with all my heart. I want to give my whole life to you. Can I just do that without reading the Bible?"

But that sense of urgency that I must read it just wouldn't go away. So, in obedience I picked the Bible up and opened it. Then to my absolute amazement, as I started reading, I understood it! I didn't have to go back and read things over again three or four times to get the meaning. The understanding came the first time. I found I could read on without stopping. It was a miracle! And you know what? Something else happened that I had never experienced with any book ever in my life. I could not put it down!

I began to cherish the Word of God. I would go nowhere without it. When I read it, the words would pulsate with life, like each word had its own heartbeat, declaring life and purpose in every sentence! For the very first time in my thirty years, I was not getting through a book; rather the book was getting through me.

I figured, if you wanted to get to know someone you should probably read their autobiography. So I picked up the Bible each day to read about HIS story! I could not find anything in the book that if applied to one's life, the universe would not be a better place. It seemed so logical and reasonable. I found God's ways to be ways of pleasantness, protection, and peace, and to this day I have never changed my opinion one iota. So I dug deep and found gold in that Book. Not only did I discover gold, but precious stones, even diamonds! Every time I read God's Word, another beautiful facet came into view and the Lord became all the more precious. I couldn't get enough! But truth be told, I was quite surprised by some of my findings, very surprised, in fact. If you will come along with me, I believe that you will be surprised as well.

I hope and pray that you will see that God is so very real. If you are a believer, I pray that God would become all the more vast to you and that the grandeur of God will never end for you. I pray that your worship will deepen, as the worth-ship of God grows. If you are not a believer, I pray that what I tell you will touch something deep in your soul to search God out, for if you search with sincerity, you will find Him. If you are on the fence, I pray that this book will catapult you over into the Kingdom of God forever!

# CHAPTER FIVE

# FINDING
# TRUTH

As I said, as soon as we arrived home, I began to do the only thing I knew to do and that was to read the Bible, A.K.A. God's Word. I thought I knew what the Old Testament said, being Jewish and all, so I thought I would delve into the New Testament. By now, I am confident that you know that all the writers of the Bible were Jewish except for one, Luke, who was probably a proselyte to Judaism. Nevertheless, the Bible records that he was a doctor, so I'm thinking there must be some Jewish lineage somewhere along the branches of his family tree. Just kidding, of course.

I had only read the Gospel according to John before. Now I turned over the last page of Malachi and began to read Matthew's Gospel account and was totally and utterly blown away by the very first line of the very first chapter. In Matthew Chapter one, verse one, in the New International Version, I read the genealogy of Jesus the Messiah. I asked myself, *Why is the word "'Messiah" being used?* "Messiah" is very Jewish terminology. I was under the impression that Jesus was referred to as "Christ". To me this appeared to be his surname, so I thought his parents were Mr. and Mrs. Christ. Then I read Jesus was the son of David, the most famous King in Israel's history. Next, I saw that Jesus was referred to as the son of Abraham, the first Patriarch of Israel! This is the very way Jews refer to God, as Abraham's God or the God of Abraham, Isaac, and Jacob! I thought, *This is crazy. Maybe it's just a fluke, or a way to allow the Jewish people to see the Jewishness of Jesus.*

But as I continued reading, I discovered that in the very next chapter Jesus was being referred to as the King of the Jews. I asked, *The King of the whose?* I was always under the impression that Yeshua had nothing to do with the Jewish people. Believe it or not, I was under the impression that Jesus was actually the leader and founder of Catholicism. This is what happens when you grow up in a neighborhood with only one huge Catholic church and one small Orthodox synagogue.

Later on, in the Gospel account, Yeshua is also called the King of Israel. I exclaimed to myself, *This can't be. This just couldn't be!* For if He was truly the King of Israel, then those who believe He is the Messiah would have to be part of the Commonwealth of Israel, no?

As I continued my very basic survey of Matthew, I couldn't help to see in chapters five through seven, Yeshua was teaching basic Torah. He was speaking on subjects like murder, marriage, divorce, oaths, stealing, etc. In fact, within the fifth chapter of Matthew itself, He states that He did not come to abolish Torah! He uses the words "abolish" and "fulfill" which was a very basic first century rabbinic augmentation. I had been under the assumption that Jesus came to nail the Law to the cross.

Later in Matthew 22, when asked what the most important commandment was, Yeshua answers with the very watchword of Israel, the Shema, Deuteronomy 6:4-5! This is spoken by devout Jews four times daily! —Twice during morning prayers, once during the evening service, and finally one more time at home before going to sleep. Although Judaism has no catechism, the Biblical verse, "Shema Yisrael Adonai Eloheinu Adonai Echad—Hear O Israel, the Lord is our God, the Lord is one" is the very heart of Judaism. It is the closest thing to being Judaism's credo. In just six Hebrew words, it sums up Judaism's belief in monotheism and its rejection of idols.

Then Yeshua continues by declaring Leviticus 19:18, the importance of loving one's neighbors, which is known as "the golden rule" within Judaism. These two commands, Deuteronomy 6:4 and Leviticus 19:18, are the two pillars holding up the Jewish faith. Love God more than yourself, and love everyone else like yourself. The rest is commentary.

After finishing the Book of Matthew, I continued on to other Gospel accounts. In Luke 2:21 I saw Yeshua getting circumcised on the eighth day. I just couldn't understand why the founder of Christianity would be obeying every Jewish law according to Torah! Circumcision is an exclusive Jewish rite. It was instituted in Genesis 17:9-13. In fact, not only is Yeshua being circumcised on the eighth day, but His counterpart John the Baptist is getting circumcised also on the eighth day. I also come to find out that John was not a Baptist, but a devout Jew in the lineage of the priests of Israel! His father was of the cohanim, the Levitical priesthood. His mother's family tree comes from the Aaronic priesthood, or the Cohane HaGadolim, the high priests! The High Priests were the only ones who had access to the Holy of Holies behind the veil and that being only once a year on Yom Kippur.

Then I saw in Luke 2:22, Miriam, Yeshua's mother, going through her rite of purification according to the Torah, Leviticus 12:1-8, another exclusive Jewish practice. In the next verse Yeshua is being dedicated, which is something Jews do as standard procedure in the Jewish community according to Exodus 13:11-15 and Numbers 18:14-16. In other words, these are typical rites and rituals followed by all who claim to be Jewish according to the laws of Moses. They are still being carried out around the world today by people of Jewish heritage!

You must understand that I was far from being a scholar, and I was no member of the intelligentsia. But, as I continued reading more and more, I began to understand why Yeshua had told me on that mountain that He never gave up being Jewish. Today when I find myself in believing circles of differing denominations, maybe at a Pastor's meeting or a prayer breakfast, there is always someone who tries to make me comfortable by saying, "Well, Rabbi Greg, Jesus was Jewish."

I always feel like saying, "What do you mean Jesus *was* Jewish? What is He now? Did He have some kind of conversion that I know nothing about? Maybe during His ascension, He became a Protestant?"

I am well aware that this may sound harsh, but Replacement Theology (which says that God is done with the Jews, that the church *replaces* the Jews, and that it is wrong to keep *Biblical* Jewish customs) is harsh. Using Replacement Theology, the adversary has done a tremendous work of destroying what the Lord had accomplished making the Jew and the Gentile one in Messiah. (See Ephesians chapter two.) The enemy is trying to rebuild the wall that Yeshua so beautifully and magnificently tore down. The fact remains. Jesus was Jewish, is Jewish, and He is coming back Jewish! He did not come to start a new religion but to complete an old one. That is why I feel "completed."

In fact, Yeshua's closest talmid (student/disciple), John, writes in his very first chapter, in verse twelve that as many as received Him, they would be made sons of God! In other words, Jews don't have to give up being Jewish; they just must recognize Yeshua as King, their King. They must confess that it was He that the prophets spoke about, that He would come down and be our Great High Priest and give His life as a ransom for many. He would be our Suffering Servant sent by God Himself, and would be made a sacrifice for all time for the atonement of sin. Yeshua did not come to die for Judaism, but for the Jewish people, as well as all people. Yeshua (Jesus) died for sins and the sinners!

Biblical Judaism is beautiful. But lying, murdering, stealing, adultery, etc. is of the enemy and only leaves a trail of tears in its wake! Sin is the great destroyer of lives. I believe that once we are housed with the Holy Spirit, we will conduct our lives differently. We will be more Jewish, not biologically but Biblically. We will be real praisers of God! (The Hebrew word for Jew—Yehuda—actually means *a praiser of God*.)

How do we praise God you may ask? By obeying His commandments! Just ask Yeshua and He will tell you what He said over 2,000 years ago in John 14:15, 21, and 23. This was when He was delivering His last will and testament. "If you love Me, you will obey Me." I have shared over 1,000 sermons, and I have heard my fair share as well. I have traveled to all but one continent sharing, preaching, and teaching. But I must tell you, the greatest sermon ever preached is an obedient life!

In the New Testament in 1 John 3:4, sin is described as lawlessness. Therefore, using some basic, deductive reasoning and overall logic, I believe that once we are born anew, we will actually be more lawful, not more lawless. As mentioned earlier, in the Bible, the prophet Ezekiel tells us that in the future God will sprinkle us with clean water, and give us a new heart. The Lord will take away our stony heart and give us a heart of flesh. The Lord will also put a new spirit inside us and *cause us* to respect His rulings, live by His laws, and obey them.

This is an incredible miracle to say the least. The Lord, through faith in the Messiah, will miraculously and magnificently give us a new receiver, so to speak. This new receiver of ours will be able to receive celestial downloads from the heavens—the Lord communicating with His creation. I would like to illustrate this point with the modern day apparatus, the GPS, the Global Positioning System. I myself do not own one, but I was riding with a friend of mine in his fancy, shmancy car and he had plugged in some destination coordinates into his GPS. Once we were off and running, the voice spoke to us and recommended that we get off the highway at the next exit in order to reach our destination. I asked my friend if he felt compelled to exit. To which he said, "What do you mean, *compelled?*"

"Well, do you have to exit or can you just keep driving?"

"Of course I could just keep driving." I then asked him what the GPS would do if he didn't exit. He said the system would instruct him to turn around to get back on course.

It was at this point that the Lord told me we have a GPS in our heart. It is God's Positioning System. The Holy Spirit will direct us in life, but it is up to us to yield to the directions. If and when we don't, we get lost. However, through the gift of repentance and God's amazing grace, we may turn around, get back on track, and get to our destination!

The Lord through His Holy Spirit sends forth directives that lead us down the path of righteousness. By the way, "righteousness" is a fancy word that means "rightness". This "rightness" in life not only brings us personal blessing, but allows us to be a channel of blessing to all those we come in contact with. I have always had a desire to do the right thing, but I struggled so, and on my own I failed miserably. But thanks be to God, who not only gives us the new receiver, but He provides the wonderful transmissions as well.

A new heart does new stuff. If you look to the Bible, you will identify with what I am saying. Each and every time an individual encountered the Messiah and recognized Him as such, they were changed! Now please understand that we do not obey God *for* our salvation, but we have a desire to obey God *because of* our salvation. I believe it was the Lord Himself who placed that very desire on our hearts. It becomes our pleasure and highest goal to obey the Lord, and we delight in His ways. We come to the conclusion that God's ways are ways of pleasantness, protection, prosperity, and peace! Who in their right mind doesn't want pleasantness, protection, prosperity, and peace? I have been to over thirty countries, and I can tell you that all people are looking for peace. If the Lord really loves us the way He says, then would He give us any directive that would potentially hurt us?

There will always be those, who sadly enough, miss the boat and operate in legalism. I believe that legalism is dangerous and quite unbecoming. However, legalism is not what you do. It's the reason behind why you are doing it! A person can pray legalistically, go to Church legalistically, and feed the poor legalistically! But if a person's obedience is birthed out of a trust grounded in faith, and rooted and founded in love, then it's kosher! You can't obey what you don't trust, and you can't trust what you don't love. You can't love what doesn't love you. So first and foremost, you must fall head over heals in love with His love, which we see on that execution stake at Golgotha. Then we fall in love with Him, He wins our trust and begets our obedience. Obedience is the key to God's heart, but love turns the key.

To find out if you are operating in love or legalism, do what I call the "fruit test". The fruit test is the litmus test for detecting the presence of legalism or heartfelt desire. Is the fruit produced from your efforts love, joy, peace, patience, kindness, etc. or is the fruit produced from your efforts envy, strife, jealousy, quarrels, and contention? This should be an excellent way for one to know if it's love or legalism.

I have been ministering for over twenty years now, and after traveling the world over I have found that people are basically people! What I mean by this is that it is a difficult task to find the fullness of the grace and the truth. I tend to meet people who move either in one camp or the other, but not necessarily in both. If you walk in grace and only grace, you may end up in licentiousness, thinking, *God loves me and He must understand, so it doesn't matter what I do.* This line of thinking can be deceptive and can lead to what Jude calls "grace abuse" in Jude 4. If you walk in truth and only truth, you may wind up living in a legalistic fashion, thinking that you are holier than most, and fail to see your own shortcomings. This line of thinking can be destructive and you may find yourself turning more folks off than on. Look out, for pride comes before a fall. So who wants to live in a destructive mode or a deceptive one?

The word of God tells us in John 1:1 that Messiah Yeshua was the Word in the very beginning, and in verse 14 it says that He took on flesh and tabernacled among us. John then makes a fantastic statement declaring that Yeshua was full of grace and truth. Did you get that? He was not 50% grace and 50% truth, but He was 100% grace and 100% truth! Hallelujah! All grace can lead to deception and licentiousness. All truth can lead to destruction and legalism. But when grace and truth meet together, and justice and peace have kissed each other, you have salvation and you have Yeshua.

## MARRIAGE AFTER THE HONEYMOON

Bernadette and I came home from Israel in 1989 two very different people. Even though now born again, we had gone through a difficult secular relationship for five years prior to getting married. There was much muddy water under the bridge and it was starting to rear its ugly waves. It was a terrible time for us, as the true love we should have had for each other was not there. I was not working and our marriage was crumbling, so it felt like my life was totally falling apart. I couldn't understand how and why this was happening. I mean, I was a follower of God now; therefore everything should be honky dory, no?

Bernadette and I ended up separating for a season. I did not want her to go, as I was really in love with her. But you see for those prior five years I had acted quite selfishly—running and moving to my own beat. I didn't realize at the time but I had hurt her very badly. She had been very much in love with me for almost all of our courting, but I lost her love because of the various antics of mine.

I told the Lord that I could not take being out of work, and having a failed marriage at the same time. I missed Bernadette desperately. I told Him that I was at rock bottom. I mean, how could a successful businessman who had the world by a string end up down and out, unemployed, and broke—with a failed marriage to boot? I told the Lord that I wanted to return to my old life. I would get a job in downtown New York, start making money again and regroup. He told me not to, that He would restore all things.

At the time I was so befuddled that I didn't even know if it was His voice or just voices in my head. I asked Him how I could know if the voice was His voice or just something I ate the night before. He told me it was Him. I then said "I need a sign because I cannot take the pain anymore from the insecurity."

He told me I would have to trust Him.

I asked, "Is that all you have for me?"

He said, "Yes, and again you will just have to trust Me."

I was out of work for about six months. I was always a frustrated athlete, so I decided to pursue what I loved. I decided to get a job in the fitness industry and to get involved with triathlons. I landed a job at a prestigious health club in Westchester, New York. I went from a six figure income to earning only $6 an hour. I trained like a banshee three times a day for the triathlons and ended up coming in first place in my very first competition.

Well, eventually, by God's grace, Bernadette and I found ourselves back together again. Thank God! When we did He told us to leave our lives behind—our friends, our families, and familiarities—and head south. So we picked up and moved to Ormond Beach, Florida. It was a delightful spot and we were looking forward to the move as it was our dream to live by the beach. But, I will never forget the pain of leaving my friends, family, and New York behind.

We learned a very important spiritual principle through our struggles together. Sometimes the Lord will bring you down to your foundation in Him and then rebuild you to a place beyond your wildest imagination. In other words, sometimes you have to tear something down before you can build it back up. That's what we had to let God do with our marriage. We found that if you let God be the builder, your spiritual house will be able to stand against the worst of storms!

## Trying to Become a Priest

The Lord told Bernadette and I to leave New York in 1992, so we made our exodus to Jerusalem west, a.k.a. Florida. We had no jobs and no friends, but we had Him. When we settled in, which took all of about two or three weeks, we felt led to find a place to fellowship. So we ended up at a small but loving church about a half-mile from our apartment complex. It was a place where people truly loved one another, and they were crazy about us. We were young, vibrant, and passionate about God.

It was an Episcopal church which I knew nothing about. The Priest took a tremendous liking to us as did the entire congregation. It was a small church so everyone knew each other fairly well. As I said, we were new in the Lord and extremely zealous for the things of His Kingdom.

The Priest had informed me that I absolutely had a call from God on my life. He had me share my testimony before the entire church and there was not a dry eye in the house. Later I became the Youth Leader where I did my best to help the young people get fired up about God.

One day in Barberville, Florida, sitting in a little ma and pa Mexican restaurant, I found myself, a New York Jew, with an Episcopal priest and a Catholic nun. It almost sounds like the start of a joke, "So there was this Rabbi, a priest, and a nun eating lunch together at a Mexican restaurant..."

I was there to help distribute some clothes to the needy, migrant, farm workers in the area. I was eating my lunch when all of a sudden I began to chuckle. Both the priest and the nun looked at me and asked, "What are you laughing at?"

I told them, "If three years ago someone would have prophesied that I would be with a priest and a nun believing in Jesus and handing out clothes to the needy, I would have thought them to be a few fries short of a happy meal!"

After working with the Episcopal Church for awhile, I began to feel called to the priesthood. So with my priest's encouragement, I was introduced to the Bishop over Central Florida. But to my great disappointment, the Bishop informed me that he did not feel I was called to become an Episcopal priest, or any priest for that matter.

Not one to give up, I later met with other church leaders to see if they thought I was priestly material. I even had an official appointment with a Bishop who was over the entire State of Florida. Each and every time, I received the same response, "Although it seems that you love the Lord, and you are quite passionate about the Kingdom, the 'professional' priesthood is not your calling." I respected their years of priestly service as well as their discernment, so I deferred to their wisdom.

## Finding the Messianic Movement

I had found a job at a local fitness center in our new home town, where I was doing my fair share of witnessing. One day I was introduced to a Jewish man, and I began to shine the Light. In our conversation he told me he was a Messianic Jew. I was familiar with the terms, Orthodox, Conservative, and Reformed Judaism, but what in the world was "Messianic Judaism"? He explained a bit and I was quite surprised as I was under the impression I was the only Jewish person who believed in Jesus!

I asked the man where he attended, and he told me Beth Judah Messianic Congregation. I told my wife we should probably visit. One Shabbat we strolled in and I could not stop crying. I felt as though I had finally come home. I was not sure about Bernadette, but she had said in regards to our new found faith, "Your people shall be my people and where you go so shall I."

I told my priest at the Episcopal Church about the Messianic Congregation. He said he knew, because of my Jewish heritage, that this was where I needed to be. Well, there you have it. Nothing in my life seems to happen by chance. It appears that the Lord is involved with everything.

By the way, my sweet, gentle mom has not yet come to know Yeshua as her Messiah, in spite of seeing all the wonderful things He has done in my life. She believes everyone should be happy. She will encourage someone even if they are doing something against the principles she believes in. She will say, "Honey, does it make you happy?" If you answer in the affirmative, she will say, "If it makes you happy, then I'm happy for you." She taught me to live by the rule, "If you have nothing nice to say, don't say anything."

However, the change in me has sent my mom back to the synagogue. She now lights the Shabbos (Yiddish for Sabbath) candles and faithfully attends services every week. She has become repentant and has turned back to God, for this I am very thankful.

# CHAPTER SIX

# ANSWERING THE CALL

Bernadette and our son, Jeremy

It was the spring of 1999 and something wonderful took place. I was called to ministry. I say wonderful because ever since my encounter with God back in 1989, I had felt I would be called to vocational ministry! The move to Florida in 1992 was part of leaving the world behind and starting anew.

There is a Hebraic study in Biblical numerology called Gematria. In the Hebrew language, all words have a numerical value and all numbers have meaning. Being a mathematician, I have always been fascinated with numbers. Gematria or Biblical numerology is right up my alley. Now it was 1999, ten years since I had received salvation in 1989, and seven years since I had left New York and arrived in Florida! Ten is the number that represents completion; and seven the number that represents spiritual perfection. So I was quite comfortable with the numeric symbolism, but I wasn't quite comfortable with what happened next.

I remember it like it was yesterday. The Elders of our Messianic Congregation came and asked me to lead our fellowship in Florida. Our congregation had been quite vibrant and had pretty decent unity. My wife and I enjoyed the people immensely. We had just completed a building project, and we were all very excited. Then sadly, our leader stepped down and left the fellowship. Unfortunately, a large number of people were hurt, and they left as well. The Bible says in Zechariah 13:7, "Strike the shepherd and the sheep scatter." We experienced this very Scripture first hand—scatter they did. First, some folks who were the movers and shakers began to leave, the entire praise and worship team followed, and then the mass exodus began! My wife and I, along with about twenty-five other committed folks, decided to stay.

It was a very sad, dark time for all of us. Spiritual divorce is very painful, to say the least. I remember asking my wife if she thought we should look elsewhere for another fellowship. I remember her saying, "I clean the toilets in this place! I'm not going anywhere!" It is not easy trying to find Messianic Rabbis, as there is not a Messianic seminary pumping them out. We are basically a newly resurrected prophetic movement from the first century, so we do not have many Jewish believers who necessarily have a desire to become Messianic Rabbis. Those who are ordained in the Messianic Movement are already quite busy leading their own congregations, so we were at a loss with no leader, no praise and worship team, and no money. One thing we did have was a big, fat mortgage.

We decided to ask another Rabbi from Jacksonville to step in and give us a hand. Our congregation met on Saturday morning, and his met on Friday evening so this was a possibility. Jacksonville was not around the corner. It was ninety miles away, but we called him anyway. We told the Rabbi our situation and found that he was already well aware of it. I've always said, "I wish that good news traveled as fast as the bad news does." He graciously agreed to help us, but after a few months, the travel and his full schedule did not allow him to continue. This is where I came in. The Elders of our fellowship met and decided to ask me if I would step up and step in and be the interim leader. They had recognized a calling on my life but truth be told, there was no one else to help, and things were getting pretty desperate. When they posed the question to me, I was completely overwhelmed and nervous, but excited at the same time.

I knew in my heart I was no Rabbi, but the Lord will use the weak and the fool at times to shame the strong and wise. I definitely fit into the weak and foolish category, so I told them that I would seek and inquire of the Lord. I got on my bicycle which was my mode of communion with the Lord. I began my ride with the Lord on a very secluded bike route that many came from far and wide to experience.

As I mentioned, I had felt deep in my heart that the Lord was calling me into ministry back in 1989, soon after my encounter in Israel, but this was an official step and I was shaking in my boots. John Wayne once said, "Courage is when you are shaking in your boots, but you still mount your horse!" I did not have a horse to mount, so I got on my bicycle and sought the Lord with all my heart.

If God said, "No", I was more than willing to back out gracefully. You don't want to do anything without the Lord's blessing, especially ministry. I was well aware that apart from Him I could do absolutely nothing, so I pleaded, "Lord, speak to me, for your child is near and listening."

I had been very involved in evangelism, prison ministry, youth ministry, and Bible teaching. Of course, I was doing this all as a layman and as a volunteer, but the anointing of God is the anointing of God. This though, was going to be a professional move as they were going to pay me a whopping $100 per week!

I began to think back to when I had met with the big wigs to talk about attending seminary to become a priest. I must tell you at this point I was confused. I said, "Okay Lord, the congregation is desperate and there are no Rabbis available. If they just need a body and I am that body, then I will go. I am not impressed with myself one iota, so if You want me to fill these shoes before You find the right person for the job, then so be it. But I would really like your blessing either way. Like King David said in Psalm 131, 'Lord my heart isn't proud; I don't set my sights too high.' So just tell me, Father, what is going on here? I can handle the truth if it's coming from You. Here I am being asked by men to serve as a leader. Is it You who is calling me, or is it them? Why did the men of God in the past tell me I wasn't priestly material and yet I am being called now?"

The Lord told me something so beautiful that day. I need to preface it by saying that He told this to me personally, and not necessarily as a universal doctrine. He told me that it was He that placed all the road blocks and obstacles that prevented me from attending seminary. I asked, "But why Lord?" He told me He wanted me for Himself. He wanted someone consecrated unto Him who would do whatever He said. I began to sob again. (Ever since I came to know the Lord and was befriended by Him, I have done my fair share of sobbing.)

I got back with the Elders right away and told them that the Lord gave me clearance and I would accept the call. It felt like another amazing experience with the Lord. I am a big fan of encounters with the Lord. I can learn a lot from others and their experiences, but I need to have my own! A God encounter will change you forever, just ask Isaiah about the time he saw the Lord high and lifted up in a vision. By the way, the prophet saw this vision just prior to his calling as well. You can read the details in the sixth chapter of the prophecy of Isaiah.

I was completely overwhelmed by the call, as I knew in my heart that I had no real idea what I was doing. I had been around the faith for ten years now, but never formally trained to be a Rabbi or Pastor. I did come to find out that the Lord doesn't call the qualified, but the Lord qualifies the called. The important issue is whether or not you are called. I have a friend who says that some were sent, and some just took the microphone and went.

The job of a Rabbi/Pastor is truly wonderful, as the Bible states, but only if it is a divine call. The Lord will always use the weak and the foolish! Why, you may ask? As I mentioned from the start, the Lord we serve and the Lord we love is incredibly merciful and loving. He does not pay us back as our sins deserve, and He overlooks more than we know. But, by the same token, He will not share His glory with, nor give His praise to another. If He uses the strong and the wise, then the strong and the wise tend to get the credit.

Just look at the story of Gideon. Coming from the least of all of Israel's tribes, the least family of the tribe, and the least member of that family, Gideon was quite afraid to take on the mighty Midianites. Not only was he overwhelmed in his heart, but then the Lord reduces his army from 32,000 fighting men to 300! If that's not enough, the Lord gives Gideon only shofars (rams horns) and lanterns as weapons. Overwhelming odds, but God!!! I believe Gideon received a faith injection through that experience that may have inoculated him from fear the rest of his days.

So here I was, going to the office, knowing in my heart of hearts that I was clueless. The only resource I had was desperation! So I would cry out to God in my humility and brokenness. These were great days, as I would feel so very close to God. There was a beautiful intimacy, as I knew I was totally and unequivocally dependent on Him. Although it was a fragile time in my life, it was a great time as well. I can only hope and pray I never forget it. I was nervous and intimidated, but excited. I came to the realization that I had received a call that came from the Lord Himself. I never, ever want to be driven by God, just led. I had always believed from the time the Lord came to me in 1989, that I was going to be involved in full time ministry. I just did not know how or when it would all come to pass. When I

The day of my ordination

103

tried to pursue it on my own, I came up short. When I gave up, it found me!

By the way, I became the Rabbi of Beth Judah just 4 years after first visiting, and the man I first spoke to, Shelly London, became my Cantor. Just for the record, Shelly was a professional Cantor for a Conservative Synagogue for over 30 years. He has an amazing gift from God for liturgy. I am indebted to him to this very day.

## My Son

Life was good. I was married to a beautiful gal—beautiful both inside and out. We had a humble little home. By the way, this was the first house that my wife and I had ever lived in, as we both grew up in apartments. Bernadette was one of six children and I was one of four. We had always shared our rooms with siblings, and even walked several blocks to get to the laundromat in order to wash our clothes. The condominium I had lived in was really just a glorified apartment. So owning our very own private house was a dream come true. We also had our first child, who, may I add, was the light of my life.

I tend to lose interest in things very easily. But there were two things that I just adored. One was spending time with the Lord. I just couldn't get enough. I would talk to Him throughout the day. I would take Him with me wherever I went. I would meditate on Him all day long, and I just loved it. The other thing I loved was being a father. It gave me a deep sense of satisfaction. I was totally fulfilled with a sense of purpose being a dad. I was completely content being with God and being with my son!

At the time of my call, my son, Jeremy, was all of five years old and we were inseparable. We did everything together. We went everywhere together. We even dressed alike. Life was good. No, life was wonderful! I had a great wife, a beautiful son, and a legitimate call to ministry. I had found peace and harmony, and it is all because of God!

One of my favorite pastimes was coming home at the end of the day. At the time, I was working two jobs. In ministry, I was what is referred to as bi-vocational. I would come home after a busy day and when I would pull up in the driveway, Jeremy would fling open the door, do a little dance, singing, "Daddy's home! Daddy's home!"

I had never experienced this kind of flagrant, wild, unrelenting, unconditional, pure love like I had from him. It made me feel like I was ten feet tall every time I came home. So my home became my sanctuary. I knew in my heart that I would have never, ever had this without the Lord! Left to my own devices, I would have been a statistic for sure. Greg could have never been happily married, selflessly parenting a child, making very little money, and been content. Financially I was poor, but spiritually I was filthy rich! The Lord had truly changed my thinking. I had a mental makeover, and I actually started to like myself, not love, but like myself. It was a great feeling and, by the way, this feeling is available for all men!

There was this one day, though, that I will never, ever forget. It will stick with me for all time. I had arrived home a few days after I received my call to the ministry, and my son did not run out to the car as usual. This day was different. The door didn't fling open, there was no song or dance, and there was no son jumping in my arms! I had this sense that something was wrong, in fact, radically wrong. I walked into the house and there was my son walking to me with stiff legs as if they were in casts. I looked at my wife and did not say a word. My facial expression said it all. She just shook her head. I took a look at his legs and I noticed these red dots all over them. I was a physical trainer at the time, and knowing my son had just begun a gymnastic program, I thought to call his instructor and inquire of any new training techniques that may have caused this condition. The instructor assured me that they had not introduced anything new.

At the time, we did not have any medical insurance but we were blessed with three very good friends who were doctors—two surgeons and one emergency room physician. They were and still are great friends of mine, and they all looked out for us. I called the ER doctor, and he came over right after his shift. I remember him looking at me and telling me that I better take Jeremy to his pediatrician. I was surprised by what our friend said, as he was very much a non-alarmist. My son had been blessed with good health for the first five years of his life. We were very health conscious, as we both came from physical training backgrounds. We ate a very healthy diet and if and when our son did get sick, we usually would let his body fight it so he could develop a strong immune system.

Although this was unusual for my friend to recommend a pediatrician, we of course took his advice and my wife made an appointment the following day. I remember the appointment was at 9:00 A.M. and I had asked her to please call the fitness center where I was working to give me the report. It was after ten o'clock and she hadn't called, so I assumed that everything was fine. "Surely my wife just forgot to call and went off to run a few errands," I told myself. "She'll call when she gets home."

At about eleven o'clock, I got concerned and called the doctor's office myself. I spoke to a nurse and I explained who I was. She told me to hold on and she would get the doctor to speak with me. I was not comfortable with this at all. I got this real queasy feeling in my stomach like something was wrong. Something was really wrong. I waited a short time, but it seemed like an eternity. The doctor got on the phone and told me that my son had a rare blood disease called ana-phylactoid purpura. I, of course, did not know what he was talking about, so I asked him to explain in layman's terms. He said it is a disease where the smallest blood vessels in our bodies, known as capillaries, break for no known rea-son. This causes swelling of the organs and joints which can be quite painful. The disease usually goes away on its own after about ninety days. He said they usually just treat the pain and swelling with anti-inflammatories, and if need be, steroids.

I thought well, this doesn't sound that bad, thank God. But then he said, "I must tell you, Mr. Hershberg, if the con-dition moves up the body, and the capillaries break in the brain, it can be fatal." As he said the word FATAL, it sounded as if the word was echoing over and over, and louder and louder in my head.

I hung up the phone and my knees began to buckle. So, I got down on my knees or should I say fell to my knees in front of my desk. I took all my pictures of Jeremy out of my wallet and placed them on the desk in front of me. I spoke to the Lord and said, "You know I love you, Lord. In fact, I am crazy about you! I know that You know what is best for me, but I don't think I could lay my Isaac down!" I knew deep in my heart I didn't deserve anything, as my dad would tell me when I was a boy, "Nothing is coming to you, kid." I truly be-lieved this. But my son! O my only son! How could I deal with him not being here with me? We had hundreds of pictures of him, but I needed more than pictures! How could I sit at our table and eat and ever enjoy mealtime again with his place missing at the table? How could I possibly go on into ministry without my son?

Yes, that was the big question. What a dichotomy! I was just called to ministry, the best day of my life, and in the same week my son was just diagnosed with a blood disease, the worst day of my life! I was struggling dealing with the two emotions at the same time. I remember saying to the Lord that I desperately needed Him. I told the Lord that I was afraid. I was afraid that if I lost my son, I may not love and trust Him anymore and thus walk away from my faith. This scared me to death. I told the Lord to keep me close to Him because I couldn't bear to lose my two best friends all at the same time!

The next day we went out to eat with a few friends. We were trying to have a good time, but I just couldn't fake it so I told them I wanted to go home. My son was always the life of the party, and so was I for that matter, but that night he was extremely quiet. I knew he was in pain so I decided to leave the restaurant. I told my friends how I felt and I motioned to my wife that I would like to go home. When I asked my son to come along, he told me he couldn't walk, so I lifted him up and he gave out a loud shout in pain. I lifted his shirt a bit and to my dismay, I noticed the red dots had traveled up to his rib cage!

Of course, you know what I was thinking. The capillaries are breaking and moving up towards the head! I grabbed my son and ran to the car, as he was crying from the pain. We arrived home and my wife took my son into our bedroom to lay him down. The house we had was small, with only two bedrooms. I went into my son's room in great pain and I threw myself on the floor crying out before the Lord. I told the Lord that I knew He loved me and I knew I loved him. I told the Lord that I believed there was nothing He couldn't do, and I was convinced that He knew all things. Then I said, "Lord, although You know all things, I believe You may not know just one thing, and that is just how much pain I'm in! For if You did, You would surely take my pain away!" I believe that anyone reading this book can relate to what I am saying, as we all have questioned God at one time or another.

That night in my son's room, I heard what appeared to be an audible voice. I'm not sure it was, in all actuality, audible, but it was so real, so clear, so much like a legitimate audible voice! The Lord said to me in that very moment, "Greg, I had a Son too." When I heard that, I was completely cut to the heart! I was crushed! I was undone!

All of a sudden, I got this incredible revelation that the Lord had suffered so much for me. No, He suffered so much for the entire world. Who are we to complain and make our demands to Him? I would not want to be God. It seems to me that when things go well, man takes the credit and when things go wrong, God gets the blame. He has given us His all, and we have given Him so little back! We live in a fallen world, and in a fallen world things fall, and sometimes, sadly enough, we get hit by some of the debris. I felt ashamed and altogether broken.

Then the Lord told me He was going to heal my son. But now I felt so ashamed that I didn't feel worthy or deserving to receive the healing. I said, "Oh God, no."

But He said, "Yes, my son."

Then I asked, "Why?"

To which He said, "Before you go into a pulpit to teach and preach about Me, you must know just how much I love My children!"

The very next morning, only the third day since they had appeared, all the red dots on my son's body were gone as well as the disease! It was a documented miracle and we have the medical records to prove it!

I had realized what Abraham had come to realize. The Lord spared my son, but did not spare His own!!! This, my friend, is why I write this book. I can't make you believe this, but if and when you do, it will change everything, and I mean everything. The disease is still in the medical books, but it isn't in my son anymore. I look forward to the day when Messiah returns and there is no sickness, no sadness, no sorrow, no suffering, and no more sin! Hallelujah!

# CHAPTER SEVEN

# A
# Conspiracy
# of
# GRACE

It was the winter of 2003 and the Lord supernaturally moved me and my family, literally overnight from Ormond Beach, Florida to Macon, Georgia! We were totally content in Florida. We now had three children. Jeremy, our healed son, was now eight. Our daughter was three and our new son was just a year old. We had a great congregation on a beautiful track of land. We had a modest home, but we were a stone's throw from the beach. When we left our windows open in the evening, we could hear the wonderful sound of the waves breaking on the sand! We had terrific friends and a very satisfying life. But God! They say if you want to make God laugh, just tell Him your plans. I have been diligently serving the Lord since 1989, and in all that time, He has never ever asked me my opinion!

I was not at all excited to leave our friends and our fellowship to come and lead a start-up fellowship meeting in a store front with only about 40 people, but sometimes the wrong way is the right way with Yahweh; just ask Moses!

My story is quite comical to say the least! Our former worship leader felt that the Lord was calling him to the Atlanta area to lead praise and worship at a newly formed congregation. We were great friends and our families were very close, so we planned a trip around Labor Day weekend 2002 to get together for some fellowship and fun. We arrived at their home in the wee hours on Friday morning. We were so excited to see each other that we began to pray for each other and more importantly just to thank God for who He is!

I was posed with a question that I will never forget. My friend told me about a newly formed Messianic fellowship that was meeting in Macon, Georgia and asked if I would like to share with them on Saturday morning. I immediately responded, "NO THANKS!" I was quite tired and desperately needed a rest, or so I thought! Then he asked if I would seek the Lord, and because I had answered without acknowledging God, I decided to go with his lead and inquire of the Lord.

I immediately heard the Lord say, "Go to Macon and share with the people there." So, Saturday morning we were en route from Atlanta to Macon!

As soon as I walked over the threshold of the entry-way of the room where the meeting was held, I heard the Lord say "Would you leave everything for Me, and come here?" When you have a close, intimate relationship with someone, you know what they are saying without them having to be too long-winded. I immediately began to sob, as I knew what the Lord was asking of me. He was saying in essence, "Son, would you leave sunny Florida, the beach, your pristine bicycle rides along the shore, your friends, and your established life and come to Macon, Georgia, where you know no one?" How do you say no to the Lord, especially when you love Him so and you are convinced that He loves you and only wants the very best for you?

Now it gets interesting! We arrived home a few days later and we knew in our heart of hearts that we were leaving! We loved the neighborhood we lived in. In fact, on one end of the block was the beautiful intra-coastal waterway known as the Halifax River in the Ormond Beach area. The other end of the block was the magnificent Atlantic Ocean where we frequently watched dolphins swim by. May I add, it was probably the cleanest stretch of beach on the Eastern seaboard of the United States.

My dream as a child was to one day live in a beach-side community and to be able to walk the beach at will. I remember when my father died, my mother and I took a trip to Miami, Beach. We left New York City in December at temperatures that would make your liver quiver to arrive in Florida complete with palm trees, sunny skies, and beautiful surf. For a kid from the inner city, this blew me away. I decided that with a little bit of luck and a lot of hard work, I would live at the beach some day. So, now in Ormond Beach I was living out that dream.

By the way, this happened to be my wife's dream as well. It's always nice when the two are one.

My wife and I both fall under the category of social butterflies. We love people and we love to engage people in conversation. We were close to just about everyone on the block except for this one individual. Let's call him Mr. X. I'm not sure why we didn't click with Mr. X. Maybe it was our faith and our desire to live our faith out loud! At any rate, when we arrived home we heard a knock on the door and it was none other than Mr. X! I was quite surprised, as in the ten years we were neighbors, Mr. X had never, ever come to our door! I greeted him and asked what I could do for him. He then said to me, "Hey Greg, if you ever want to sell your house, I'd buy it." I couldn't believe my ears, so I asked him to repeat himself. He did, and I immediately asked if I could get back with him.

He left and I proceeded to recount the conversation to my wife. She was convinced that we were moving to Macon before we arrived back to Florida, but someone had to be the Jonah! I thought maybe it was a dream and I would just wake up and find we were not moving after all. Since I came to the realization that I was not dreaming, I decided I would search for a legal, spiritual loophole to circumvent leaving the dream life. I needed to think, so where does Greg go to think? The beach, of course!

There was this pool on the beach at a condominium just a few minutes from my house where a friend lived. So I loaded up the car and I took my children to the pool. The pool was usually empty, but when we arrived there was actually one other person on the pool deck. As I got closer to him I said hello and noticed he was wearing a T-shirt with an inscription that read "Welcome to Macon." I couldn't believe my eyes! I walked over to where he was sitting and asked the gentleman if he had ever visited Macon. He told me he lived in Macon but he was in Florida for a family reunion. So we came back home and I told my wife, "You're not going to believe this!"

She said, "Try me."

I'm not the sharpest tool in the shed, but I'm no bowling ball either. I was sensing that it was going to be real hard to get out of this one. But I would not give up easily. My wife would bring home boxes to pack our belongings for the in-evitable move to Macon, Georgia, and I would get rid of them when she wasn't looking! While I was still searching for a way to avoid the move, I was invited to a pastor's meeting in Orlando. When I went, I felt led to sit at this one particular table. Once I got comfortable, I turned to the pastor seated next to me and asked how he was doing and where he was from. To which he answered, "Macon".

I said, "What in the world are you doing in Orlando?" He told me he grew up in Tallahassee, Florida, but was born in Macon.

I will never forget what he said after that. He told me that he never, ever says he is from Macon. He always says Tallahassee, and he didn't know why he said Macon. He add-ed, "Isn't that weird?" I told him what was going on, and he said, "You'd better pray real hard, son."

Well, it was obvious at this point that the Lord was mov-ing us, so we accepted the call and we traveled back to Ma-con in November to find a place to live. We were looking to rent an apartment for about six months, basically a short-term lease. We looked everywhere, but there were no apart-ments available unless we were willing to lease the unit for a full year. Dejected a bit, we came back to the motel to think it over.

It was a rainy, gloomy day in Macon. The children were a bit rambunctious stuck in this rather shabby motel room. I wanted so badly to just go home to Florida and take the kids to the beach, or to get on my bike and ride down the shore and see my friends.

Suddenly I thought to myself, *Eureka! I have found my loophole. We can't find an apartment that will grant us a short-term lease.* I said to my wife, "Maybe the Lord is letting us know that this move is not His will." After my wife finished laughing, I told her with a tear in my eye that I just wanted to go back home to Florida.

She told me that Florida was no longer our home. She reminded me, "We have already accepted the position and agreed to come in January, and we don't have time to dillydally!! So we need to find a place to live before we leave to go back to Florida!"

At this point I got frustrated and blurted out a really dumb statement. I said, "If God really wants us to live here, then let Him find us a place to live!"

No more than one minute later the phone rang in the motel and my wife was conversing a bit with a smile on her face. She handed me the phone and said, "Jonah, it's for you!"

Lo and behold, it was a lady on the phone who was someone's personal assistant who did not attend the fellowship. Somehow this person heard about us and our situation and offered us their lake house. I told her, "We cannot afford to rent a home, especially one on a lake."

She responded, "Who said anything about rent? The home is a gift along with all the costs associated with the dwelling."

I had made an agreement with the Lord some time ago that if He would make things obvious to me and there was absolutely no shadow of a doubt, that I would follow His lead. Well, once again I experienced the faithfulness and goodness of Almighty God as He made this move exceptionally clear! I must tell you, though, that once I knew with clarity that it was God's desire for us to take over the congregation in Macon, I still had some reservations.

Once we returned back to Florida after finding our temporary residence in Macon, I went to the beach to commune and fellowship with the Lord. I asked Him point blank if I had to go to Macon and leave Ormond Beach, to which he said very gently but emphatically, "No, of course not."

I was relieved and yet I felt like something was wrong. I heard this loud, awkward, heavenly silence. Sometimes this silence can be deafening. So I asked the Lord, "What if I don't go and I stay here in Florida?"

He said, "Not only will your destiny be hampered, but we will not be as close as we could be, son."

Well, that was all I had to hear. So, Jonah and the family were off to Nineveh, I mean, Macon. We had said all of our goodbyes and frankly, I wasn't sure I could physically shed any more tears as we drove with our moving truck at sunrise out of Ormond Beach. I was convinced that this may not be the best move, but I was determined to prove to God that I loved Him! I have never visited the "deep south" so I really didn't know what to expect. I mean Macon, Georgia is right smack in the middle of the Bible belt.

Once we arrived in Macon and got a bit immersed in the culture, I felt as if Macon was not only in the Bible belt, but it could be considered the very buckle with more churches per capita than any other locale in the grand old USA. I must tell you, I was a tad intimidated to reside in a place where New York Jews were somewhat of an anomaly. But if God is for us, who could be against us?! I had experienced, even encountered, the miraculous hand of God many times in the past, so this would just be another opportunity for God to show Himself.

After a six hour drive from Florida, we arrived at the house that was to be our temporary residence on Lake Sinclair in Milledgeville, Georgia. We had no idea where we were, and we had no idea how to get around. I was completely unfamiliar with the area, being almost an hour from Macon. We had all of our furniture and belongings placed in storage and we arrived at the house with a few bags filled with clothes and some other minor belongings. As I sat there, I realized that the house had no telephone, no computer and no television. With all our belongings in plastic bags, a wife and three children ages 8, 3, and 1, I thought to myself, *Greg, what in the world have you done?*

In that state of mind, after discovering the house had all kinds of fisherman's gear, I decided to try my hand at fishing since there wasn't much else we could do. I had been a fisher of men for well over ten years already, so I thought it couldn't be too hard. But as I related earlier, all I have to show for it is a funny catfish story.

We decided to put our tent pegs deep into Macon, so we purchased a house and have come to feel very much at home in this place where God has planted us.

# CHAPTER EIGHT

# BECOMING DESPERATE

: Our family in Israel on the Transfiguration Mount
also known as Mount Tabor

It was Monday, October 10, 2005. We now had four children: Jeremy, eleven; a five year old daughter, a three year old son; and now a five month old baby girl. We had just returned from a family vacation. I was in my office early in the morning seeking the Lord, trying to receive my marching orders for the day! By the way, I would highly recommend seeking the Lord first thing! Yeshua taught in Matthew 6:33, "Seek the Kingdom first," which includes the King Himself, of course. Our lives are so very busy, therefore we must prioritize. I believe beyond a shadow of a doubt, that we will always make time for the things that are important to us, or shall I say, the things we love. It isn't easy to get a person to fall in love with God! However, I believe the more we know and understand about the Lord, the more we will fall in love with Him. To know Him is to love Him. And the more you know Him the more you will love Him. Being that God is love, how could you not?

Well, here I was in my office very early reading, praying, and meditating on the Lord. When all of a sudden, I began to sob and wail because I realized that I was not desperate enough for the Lord. Sure, you could say that you are desperate, but truth be told in reality, many of us are not. My office was in my home at the time because our congregation had no sanctuary or facility of its own. I called my wife into my office, and told her I needed to talk to her right away. She asked me, "What is it?" She was not taken aback by my tears, as she has seen me cry many, many times before.

I told her, "I am not desperate."

"What do you mean?"

"I'm just not desperate!"

"What are you talking about, Greg? You evangelize all the time. You preach and teach the Word of God. You go into the prisons and visit with the inmates. You go off to far away lands and help the widow, the poor, and the orphan."

"I understand what you are saying, Honey, and I whole-heartedly appreciate it. But I still believe I am not truly desperate!"

If you look up the word "desperate" in the Hebrew language, it is "Aw-Nash". It means *to be weak, to be sick, or to be frail.* In the Webster's dictionary, it means *having an urgent need, or afflicted and enduring toils and troubles.*

I felt as though all things considered, my life was overall good. I had a beautiful family, a vibrant ministry, a house, two cars, and food in the fridge! Maybe I was just having trouble trying to explain myself, but at any rate I knew in my heart of hearts that I wasn't desperate.

As my wife walked out of my office, I went upstairs to shower and get ready for the day. In the shower, I heard the Lord tell me that I was to call a friend of mine who happened to be the directing physician of the emergency room in Macon, the only trauma center hospital between Jacksonville, Florida and Atlanta, Georgia. He is a very busy man so when I called him on his cell phone, I couldn't believe I reached him—at the very first attempt, no less. He mentioned to me that he was en route to the hospital returning from a weekend at his getaway home. I asked if we could have dinner some night and he said, "What about tonight?"

I, of course, responded with a resounding, "Yes!" He told me that he could pick me up at my house since the hospital is in the city, and he and I lived on the outskirts of town. I, of course, saw the logic in this, so I said, "Sure Doc."

He responded, "I'll see you at about six."

When I hung up the phone, I heard the Lord say, "You have to meet him at the hospital." So I immediately called him back and told him that I would rather meet him at the hospital.

He then replied, "That doesn't make any sense, since I have to pass by your house on the way home." I agreed, but I mentioned to him that the Lord told me I had to meet him at the hospital. My friend, being a sold out, God guy, said, "No problem, I'll see you at the hospital around six."

I arrived at the hospital at about six o'clock feeling great and looking forward to a good time of food and fellowship with my good friend. When I arrived in the emergency room, I gave Doc a big hug and he proceeded to introduce me to some of his colleagues. He asked how I was, and I responded, "Great!" I had just returned from vacation and was feeling rather rested.

He asked again, "Is everything alright?"

I replied, "Well, I do have somewhat of a pain in my lower abdomen, but it's minor so no worries. Let's go eat."

My doctor friend asked, "What do you think it is?"

"Probably a hernia," I responded.

"Let's find an examination room and I'll take a look."

To which I replied, "I will be going to Israel next month, so I would not have it repaired until I get back anyway. So let's hold off on the examination, and just go out to eat."

He said, "Come on, it will just take a minute," So we hunted around for an empty examination room. When we finally found one, he asked me to get up on the table and lie down on my back. I loosened my belt buckle and he began the examination.

When he was finished, he looked up at me and said, "Rabbi, I have some bad news for you, Buddy."

"What is it Doc?"

"You have an aneurysm!"

I asked, "Does that mean we can't go out to eat?"

"You don't know what an aneurysm is, do you?

To which I replied, "No." He explained it to me using a bicycle tube as a metaphor. He told me the bicycle tube is like your abdominal aorta, the huge artery going from your heart to your lower body. A bicycle tube can sometimes have

127

a defect or a weakness in its wall and cause it to expand in a specific locale. If it continued to expand, it would burst and lose all of its air. If the aorta, burst, instead of air, it would lose precious blood. I would have ninety seconds to live as I would bleed out and die.

I asked Doc what the procedure would entail. He told me that they would have to do an ultrasound to help determine the size of the aneurysm. If the aneurysm was five centimeters or smaller, they would monitor it to make sure it doesn't grow. If it was larger than five centimeters, they would have to do immediate surgery to repair it. I asked what was involved with the surgery and he explained just how intense the repair was, and how it involved at least five hours of surgery. He added that there was a significant mortality rate associated with this particular surgery. He told me the abdominal aorta was behind my intestines, so my intestines would have to be removed, and I would have to be placed on a life support machine so the aneurysm could be grafted. It all seemed so serious and so over the top! I mean, I just got back from a vacation and all. I was just looking forward to having sushi with my doctor friend. It all seemed a bit surreal.

When they did the ultrasound, I was just hoping they would find out the aneurysm was less than five centimeters. Well, the ultrasound was performed and, sadly enough, it turned out to be eight centimeters. They decided to perform another test called an arteriogram with a die contrast to determine not only the actual size but the exact location as well.

The test was complete and, to the doctor's surprise, they found that the aneurysm was actually about twelve centimeters. This was the biggest aneurysm they had ever seen! It was twelve by eight centimeters! Doc told me they would have to do surgery immediately as this situation fell under the umbrella of a medical emergency.

At this point, I called up my two very good friends in

Florida who happen to be surgeons and they both said they have never ever heard of a person with a twelve by eight centimeter aneurysm who survived! Well, that was quite re-assuring, so I called my wife and she asked me, "Are you having a good time at dinner?"

"I am not at dinner, Honey. I'm in the hospital and I have an aneurysm."

"What?" Needless to say, she was shocked. I explained and she said she would find a babysitter and come straight to the hospital. Bernadette and I tend to try and laugh when-ever we can, so when she arrived, she said, "Well, you sure do things in a big way, even in your illness!"

I was admitted to the hospital and you know what? Now I was desperate! Can you imagine that? Just twelve hours prior, I had begged the Lord that I would know desperation. Be careful of what you ask for, you just might get it!

They discovered the aneurysm late Monday evening. The next day they did all types of pre-operative procedures to prepare me for the surgery as well as check for any po-tential complications. The surgery was scheduled for 7 A.M. Wednesday.

Wednesday morning arrived, and I said goodbye to my four children. That was one of the hardest things I had ever done—to say goodbye to them not knowing if I would see them again. This being such a high risk surgery I wasn't sure where I was going to end up. It was either the recovery room or the resurrection room!

I asked to see the surgeon prior to the surgery. I wanted him to see my wife anointing me with oil. I asked if he was a believer, to which he said he wasn't. I asked if he was a good doctor, to which he said, "Yes." I asked him if I could anoint him. I told him that I do not easily get offended, and if he was not comfortable, he was under no obligation whatsoever. He said it would be alright, so I began to anoint his hands. I thanked God for this surgeon that he was willing to sacrifice so much to learn his craft! I told the surgeon that he need not worry if anything goes wrong. I told him that I was 46 years old and I have never been in a court of law. I told him I did not believe in lawsuits, so he should rest assured. I told him I was convinced that he would do his very best. I then asked the Lord if He would use my situation to declare the reality of His existence to this surgeon. At this point, I saw a tear in the surgeon's eye and he said he had to go.

I kissed my precious wife goodbye and was wheeled into the operating room. The weird thing was that I was placed on this wooden cross, so to speak, naked and strapped down. It was a bit surreal, if you know what I am driving at here! The very next thing I remember, I was waking up in a recovery room. It appeared that the surgery was successful and I should be home in about three to five days!

The surgeon came to visit with me the next day and told me the surgery went perfectly. He said it was the best aneurysm surgery he had ever performed. However, to everyone's shock, three days later my abdomen began to distend. They thought that maybe I had a bowel obstruction. The surgeon came to visit me and said, "I don't understand. Everything that could have gone wrong is now going wrong!"

By Tuesday of the following week, they rushed me back in the operating room, and split open the incision which goes from my chest to my groin area. I don't remember any of this. Everything went wrong after they opened me up. My intestines jumped out from my abdomen, and I aspirated, which means the fecal matter which is supposed to come out from the rectum went up my esophagus and down my trachea into my lungs. This is known to kill at least 50% of the patients. By the grace of God, I survived the surgery and the aspiration, but I was not improving.

I was in ICU for over a week. I had C-dificile colitis along with a host of other issues. I was being visited by heart doctors, lung doctors, a doctor from the CDC, etc. I could not breathe very well on my own, as my lungs were compromised by the aspiration and I had no use of my left leg because a nerve was nicked during the second surgery. I was in the hospital for seventeen days and I was not getting any better. I had no food and no water for seventeen days. I could not walk on my own. I had a massive gastrointestinal infection and could not control my bowels.

You have to realize I was a triathlete and had been a personal trainer for a long time, so this was all new to me. I was beginning to wonder what was really going on here. I tried desperately to hang onto my faith. I kept witnessing to many people during my stay in the hospital while hanging onto the Lord with all I had.

Bernadette says this about the whole experience. "Initially, upon hearing the news of the aneurysm, I was shocked and not sure how it would turn out. But after praying hard about the situation I felt God was telling me Greg would be fine and pull through. It got a little harder to believe this after the complications following what appeared to be a successful surgery. After Greg ended up in the ICU, there was a time that I cried out to God telling him I didn't want to become a widow at such a young age with small children to raise alone. But He assured me again Greg would pull through. I remember going to see him every day and trying to be upbeat and happy. I would massage his feet and attend to his needs while I stayed with him in his room. It really was heartbreaking to see him in such physical distress. He wanted so badly to get out of that hospital. Greg loves the outdoors, it was torture for him to be cooped up inside like that."

On the seventeenth night, I began to struggle. I cried out to the Lord and told Him I desperately needed to hear from Him. He spoke to me that night and told me that three times the enemy had come to try and take me out and He had stood between me and the enemy each and every time! He said I would live and I would be going home tomorrow! I asked, "How could I be going home tomorrow so sick and afflicted?"

God said, "Don't you worry. You are going home tomorrow!"

Tomorrow came and I truthfully did not feel any better than the day before. But sure enough, a student nurse came into my room and said, "Rabbi Hershberg, you're going home today!"

I said, "No offense, dear one, but shouldn't one of the many doctors that I have been seeing give me the release?" She said she had the orders to take out my three intravenous lines, my NG tube, remove my nasal breathing apparatus, and send me home. So, in came a wheelchair, along with six prescriptions and an oxygen tank, then off I went. I remember crying the whole way home. I had not been able to drink any water for eighteen days. I couldn't shower for those eighteen days. I couldn't brush my teeth for eighteen days. I couldn't even control my bowels, sadly enough.

But I was going home and God was right once again. Bernadette says, "It was an amazing day when Greg was released. It came out of nowhere. We didn't see it coming at all. But, we didn't ask any questions when they said he was free to go. We just packed up his things and got out as fast as we could before they could change their minds."

None of the children knew I was coming home, so it was going to be a surprise. Bernadette helped me up the stairs and the first one to see me was my five year old daughter. She looked up at me and with a tear in her eye, she said, "I knew you'd be coming home, Daddy." I thought that it was just one of those cute little statements that would naturally come out of the mouth of a five year old. But the Lord impressed upon my heart that it was not just your typical five year old remark. So I asked her how she knew, because I myself hadn't known! She told me very emphatically that every night she would pray to the Lord and ask him to heal me, and the Lord would tell her He was going to heal me and bring me home!

It was a very long, uphill battle I had ahead of me. Here I was, never taking a prescription medication in my life, and now I had six. I had been a triathlete, and now I needed an oxygen tank to follow me around. I also had very limited use of my left leg. Bernadette wrote to some friends in Florida telling them she was used to seeing me ride my bike forty miles, now I got tired just walking to the bathroom.

It was a desperate time, but I have never felt so close to God in all my life, except for maybe that day in Israel on the Transfiguration Mount when He first appeared to me! Now He was making His presence more real and more manifest than ever before. I felt such intimate fellowship with Him, like we were one. I would walk a bit every day, as a doctor friend of mine advised me, "Don't wait to get better to walk, but walk to get better." Every person I came in contact with, I witnessed to and I mean everyone.

Bottom line, God answered my prayers and I learned first hand what it means to be desperate! I'm not saying that it was all fun and games, but what I am saying is that it was intensely difficult and yet wonderfully great! I will never, ever forget just how great God is! You come to this realization when you are desperate.

The truth of the matter is, we are all desperate! Should photosynthesis not take place, then the trees would not produce oxygen! We are desperate to the Lord for every breath we take. It only seems right to take some of that inhalation that the good Lord provides and exhale His praises!

I hope and pray you don't necessitate life-threatening illness to see just how spiritually desperate you really are. Take nothing for granted and know that all good gifts are from the Father of lights! I would recommend we never overestimate our own goodness, and we never underestimate our own sin.

Oh, before I forget, one month later I went back to see the surgeon. I asked him, "May I ask you a personal question?"

"Go ahead."

"Did you think I was going to die?"

"Yes."

"Were you prepared to tell my 38-year-old wife, as well as my four little children that their daddy didn't make it?"

"Absolutely not!" I then asked him if he remembered my prayer to which he said, "I remember you praying, but I don't remember what you prayed."

I reminded him that I asked the Lord if He would use this surgery to show the surgeon that He existed! I asked him if he has ever seen an aneurysm that large, especially in someone so young. He, of course, said "No!" I then asked him if he had ever seen a surgery go so well, and then in his own words, seen everything that could go wrong, go wrong. He again said, "No!" Last but not least, I asked if he would be willing to admit that he did everything right, and he could not explain why everything went wrong? To which he said emphatically, "Yes!"

I then said, "Maybe, just maybe, the Lord was trying to reveal Himself to you." No response!

I believe God was giving the surgeon a chance to come to grips that He was real and that he is helpless without Him. The Lord was also giving me a chance to see how great He is once again, and just how desperately I really need Him. I truly believe that the Lord will bring good from all things for those who love Him and are called for His purposes!

So is it a bad thing to be desperate? It all depends on your perspective! If we are talking in the natural realm, then maybe one can answer yes. But if we are talking in the spiritual realm, then the answer is unequivocally, undeniably, and positively a resounding NO!!! Desperation is spiritually beautiful.

I believe in order to worship God the way He deserves to be worshiped, or better yet the way His attributes command and demand our worship, we have to have a Gethsemane experience, where we can turn to no one or no thing, except the Lord. I believe the Lord wants to be our Knight in shining armor coming to our rescue. In order for this to happen, we need to be the damsel in distress. So the next time you find yourself locked up in a tower, surrounded by alligator infested waters, guarded by the fire-breathing dragon, just cry out to the Lord and see if His hand of redemption is long enough to save you. For he who calls on the name of the Lord shall be saved!

Bernadette and I on a ministry
trip to Wales and Ireland

# CHAPTER NINE

# THE FINAL ANALYSIS

Blessing the Kingdom workers in India

As I mentioned from the start, I never intended to write a book. Then again, I never intended to become a believer in Yeshua and go around the world teaching and preaching the Word of God either! The Scripture in Isaiah 55:8 that says, "'Your ways are not MY ways', says the Lord," really has legitimate meaning for yours truly. After much prayer, and just as much confirmation, I decided to finally say yes to God.

There are thousands upon thousands of books out there that feed the Christian community. I was hoping that this book would not only bring glory to God, edification, exhortation, and consolation to my believing brothers and sisters around the world, but would also inspire those who don't yet believe to ask the question, "Are you really real, God?"

In this world that we live in, nothing is free these days. It seems like all gifts have some sort of strings attached to them. I mean, who in the world would spend so much time with total strangers to share the love, grace, and mercy of our great God and not necessarily look for anything in return? My answer is that there are no folks on the planet more unselfish, loving, and compassionate than "true" believers! True believers share because they love God and they love people and ask for nothing in return. I think that is beautiful.

I have friends in India that put their own lives and the lives of their families on the line daily just to share God's gift of salvation with folks they don't even know. There is only one thing that still remains free of charge with no strings attached. It is the wonderful, incredible, good news that although we were robbed of our excellence back in the Garden of Eden, the Lord mercifully, gracefully, and lovingly is looking to restore it. He wants to give back to us what the locusts have devoured in our lives.

If a speeding car was barreling down the road directly in your path and you were somewhat oblivious, and I moved you out of the way, what would you say to that? Better yet, what if I only had time to move you out of the way, but I had to remain in the way and take the hit? Moving you out of the way is God's way of showing His mercy and grace. But since the Lord is also just, someone does have to take the hit and pay the price. This is His truth and justice. His mercy and grace is that He took the hit! The Lord has displayed His love for thousands of years by not paying us back according to what we truly deserve. I think if we were honest with ourselves, we would agree that our trials will never exceed our transgressions.

I was speaking with someone this morning that I had just met. I love to talk to people about life, love, and the Lord! I believe the body of believers has it backward somewhat. We try to bring people to our church buildings and try and share with them God's great gift of love and salvation. But instead of bringing them to the "Church", we need to see ourselves as the "Church", and bring it to them! That's why in Mark 16:15 (NRSV) Yeshua said, "Go into all the world." He said that a city on a hill cannot be hidden. He said to shine our light before all men, and opportunities present themselves to do just that all day long.

At any rate, this was just another typical morning where I was prepared to shine the light. I met a stranger (for the time being), a young lady at a fitness center, and we struck up a conversation. I introduced myself and shared some personal information so she would not feel as though I was a complete stranger anymore. I then asked some questions about her so we could feel a sense of connection. This always leads up to the main event, God, religion, etc. It got to a point in the conversation where the Holy Spirit led me to ask this individual how she felt about God and faith. She did not at all seem taken aback, and told me she believed in God but had nothing at all to do with organized religion, like it was the plague or something. I asked, "Why?"

She said, "God was the Creator, but man created religion. All religion is man-made."

I asked, "How do you feel about the faith spoken about in the Bible?" She admitted to me that she had never ever read the Bible because she didn't believe in it. I told her that it is really unfair to comment on a book that she had never read for herself.

I asked if she had a certain creed that she lived by. She then asked, "What do you mean by creed?"

I explained, "A creed is simply a set of rules and beliefs to which a person conducts their life."

She said, "Of course I have a set of beliefs. Everyone does." I then asked if she would be willing to share her beliefs with me, for I was both curious and interested at the same time. When she finished sharing, I asked the person if she realized that she had created her very own religion.

The word "religion" comes from a Latin word which means to bind ourselves to something based on a certain set of beliefs. Everyone is religious to a certain extent, for everyone has a creed that they believe in, and this creed produces their character, not the other way around.

I then asked her, "Should I believe in your creed or should you believe in mine?

She answered, "It is all relative." I agreed although I am not a fan of relativism, which is a theory that states morals and truth are not absolute.

I asked this person, "May I share a quick story with you in connection with the theory of relativism? She indulged me and off I was running with the light. I told her that eight years ago I lived in Florida where we had a very vibrant prison ministry. We would go to the prison on Friday evenings and spend time with the inmates, believers and non-believers alike. It lasted about three years prior to us moving to

Georgia where we currently have a prison ministry as well.

The chaplain of the prison informed me that you should never ask the inmates why they were incarcerated, as this might bring bias and compromise to the ministry. This one particular night an inmate asked me if I wanted to know what he was in for, to which I replied, "No." He then proceeded to volunteer the information, telling me he was in for killing his wife for burning his dinner. He said it without remorse. I'm not a psychologist, but I wondered how hard a person's heart must be to kill someone so close to them and show no remorse! How could someone in their "right" mind not have any remorse for murdering their spouse?

I then was led by the Lord to ask the prisoner what he would do if a pedophile came into the prison, to which he said quickly, and angrily, "I'd kill him!"

You must understand that, sadly enough, a large population of prisoners are themselves victims of pedophilia. This guy showed no remorse for the murder of his own wife, but as far as he was concerned, having sex with children is wrong! Everyone has their own ideas about right and wrong and this heinous murderer had his own concept of right and wrong as well.

This is how I described relativism to the young lady I was conversing with. Although it was a very raw example, I think the point was well taken. I reasoned further. "So, if there is a God, maybe, just maybe, He has absolutes about right and wrong, too. Wouldn't you agree? And by extension, isn't it really God's absolutes that a decent society is based on?" She didn't have much to say after that. I feel confident that I influenced her to start reconsidering her beliefs. I still see her now and then and I still share with her. Many people I have introduced to the Lord are now heavily involved in ministry. But sometimes it takes time.

All of my life, I was searching for what I would call the truth. I knew it was out there, I just didn't know where it was. I was desperately trying to find out what I could expect from life, and what life expected of me. I was raised by parents, both hard working law abiding citizens, who taught principles of right and wrong.

As I said I grew up in the low income housing projects in New York City. This was a blessing, as low income families were awarded a lower rental and free utilities in order to make ends meet. I recall one day leaving the light on in my room. My father took notice and told me, "Son, shut the light off."

To which I replied, "But we're not paying for electricity."

He replied sternly, "Shut off the light, Son! Someone is paying for it." What a great concept of right and wrong! It somehow has gotten lost in our modern day thinking! Today we believe we should have everything coming to us. How sad.

As I said, I was searching my entire life, but I don't think I knew exactly what I was searching for. I figured if I found it, I would know. My mother would tell me, "Don't try and look for the love of your life, and it may just find you."

"But how will I know, Mom, when in fact I find the love of my life?"

"Oh, son," she would say, "you'll just know!"

So maybe it was love I was looking for, but I have come to the conclusion that the only true love is God's love.

Deep down inside we all want to do the "right" thing, but we struggle when we try on our own. The God of the Bible, the God of Abraham, Isaac, and Jacob has provided us with teachings, precepts, and commandments that if followed, you would be hard pressed to find even one that would not improve and change the world for the better. I truly believe that when we say yes to God, we change the spiritual complexion of the entire universe for the better.

There is a mysterious miracle that takes place when we are immersed in Messiah Yeshua for the forgiveness of our sins. Not only are our sins erased from our account, but we are the proud recipients of the "new" heart like Prophet

Ezekiel tells us about in the 36th chapter of his wonderful prophecy.

The big question though is this. Is Yeshua, in fact, the prophesied Messiah? To answer this question we can actually consult the scientific community. Science has a method of studying odds. It is called the Science of Compound Probabilities, a mathematical study of situations and the odds of possible outcomes. Professor Peter Stoner, Professor Emeritus of Mathematics and Astronomy, Pasadena College, conducted a study in his book entitled, *Science Speaks*. The purpose of the study was to determine the odds of one man in history fulfilling all the prophecies recorded in Scripture that are Messianic prophecies. A prophecy is a statement that is declared as a divinely inspired prediction, instruction, or exhortation. It is a foretelling or a prediction of what is to come. The Holy Scriptures, known as the Bible, are approximately 25% prophetic. The specific prophetic messages that relate to the Messiah, His life, His ministry, His death and His resurrection number 333. That means that in order to claim to be Messiah, the person would have to fulfill all 333 prophecies! And Yeshua did just that!

Because the odds of one man fulfilling all 333 are absolutely and ridiculously astronomical, Stoner simply chose only eight prophecies. They are as follows:

(1) Micah 5:2 - which prophecies the Messiah's birth (2) Daniel 9:25-26 - which prophecies the time of Messiah's death (3) Isaiah 7:14 - which prophecies the manner of Messiah's birth (4) Zechariah 11:12-13 - which prophecies Messiah's betrayal (5) Psalm 22:16-18 - which prophecies the conditions surrounding Messiah's death (6) Zechariah 12:10 - which prophecies the manner of Messiah's death (7) Psalm 22:7-8 - which prophecies the mocking of Messiah and (8) Isaiah 53:9 - which prophecies the Messiah's burial.

The compound probability of just eight prophecies being fulfilled by one man is 1 in 10 to the 17th power, or 1 in 100 quadrillion. To understand this number, take that many silver dollars and lay them on the face of Texas which is 267,000 square miles. This many silver dollars would cover the entire state two feet deep! Next, mark one single silver dollar and fly over Texas and drop it anywhere your little old heart desires. Then blindfold someone and let him parachute in over the state of Texas anywhere he wants. He should take his time, as he only gets one pick, and the coin he picks must be the one you marked. What are the chances of him getting the right one? You guessed it! One in 100 quadrillion!

The point Dr. Stoner is making is since the likelihood of anyone satisfying just eight is so ridiculously high, what are the chances of one man satisfying 333? Maybe, just maybe, the Lord made the outcome so ridiculously astronomical, so there would be no impostors or impersonators, just the real thing!

For 1,400 years, the Lord provided the children of Israel with a sacrificial system to pay for their wrongdoings. The sacrificial system was set up to let Israel know that sin carries a huge cost and must be paid for by an innocent victim who would have to suffer for the sins of others. If you think about it, the only part of God's creation that sins is us! It appears that the Lord was saying that sin or wrongdoing could not be overlooked nor excused, but must be paid for!

God in His infinite mercy would provide a "victim". One would think that we would look at these poor defenseless animals and feel a sense of guilt which would create an inward desire in our hearts to do the "right" thing. I can just see Adam's knees buckle when he saw that animal skin from the first sacrificed animal, thinking, *It is because of what I have done that this animal had to die.* Adam had never seen death before, so it must have been a horrible shock to him.

But as always, we humans tend to take things for granted. The animals became less important in our minds, so we didn't feel so bad after a while. I mean, they're just animals! But what if this system which was supposed to pull at our heart strings, would all of a sudden get amplified? What if the Lord raised the stakes and sent the fullness of Himself in human form as the Messiah, the Savior of the world? Well, if you check the Scriptures this was the plan! The plan came to fruition just as the Bible predicted, and it has been transforming the lives of many ever since. What began with a rag tag group of twelve regular Jewish guys in Jerusalem has turned into one billion strong and still growing as we speak!!!

You know, I think it disturbs God when we show no remorse for our wrongdoings, just like it disturbs us to think about that prisoner who has no remorse for murdering his own wife. The other week a fifteen year old kid came to me after the synagogue service. He started crying hysterically. Mucus even started coming out of his nose. He was woefully remorseful. In between sobs, he said, "Rabbi, I'm a sinner, but I want to accept the Lord's sacrifice."

The Lord is just waiting for you to appropriate and activate what He so graciously has given. But you can't save what's not drowning. So if after studying all the prophecies and looking into the bibliographical evidence as well as the external evidence to the reliability and authenticity of the Bible you still don't believe, I am ever so hopeful that the testimony brought forth in this book will help to put you over the edge and catapult you into the Kingdom.

You hear these testimonies about people who were either in jail, strung out on drugs and alcohol, going through a divorce, dealing with an inoperable illness, or maybe feeling like suicide was the only answer to life's problems and then they found the Lord. For me, this was not the case at all. I grew up in the projects raised by two wonderful parents, who loved their four children dearly as I told you earlier. There came a time when I began to meditate a bit on life. Something seemed radically wrong, although I thought I was on top of the world. My family and my friends were so proud of me and yet deep down inside there was something missing.

I believe we are like sheep who have gone astray and have lost our way. Life could and should be better, and we think we can operate on all cylinders. I've come to the conclusion that "stuff" is overrated, in fact, way overrated. Money cannot buy a person love.

So here I was asking, seeking, and knocking in my search for wholeness, peace, and satisfaction. I thank God for cognitive thinking and deductive reasoning. I said to myself, "Self, would I feel a greater sense of accomplishment if instead of three investment condominiums, I acquire a fourth?" Of course, the answer was absolutely not. "So what am I missing then?" I asked.

Well, as elaborated on earlier in this book, through a chain of events that only the Creator and Sustainer of the Universe could pull off, I found myself married and honeymooning in the land of the Bible. I thought, *What in the world am I doing here anyway?* Then literally out of the blue, the Lord found me! It was He who drew near and paid me a holy visitation. One in which I will never ever forget. I will forever be grateful to Him for making me whole. It has not always been a smooth ride. Life has its fair share of turbulent events. But all things considered, the landing will be like a butterfly touching down with sore feet.

I say all this to express that this is not your typical salvation story! But this is the way it happened. The Lord has been good to me all these years. He has taken me to six continents and thirty countries to share His good news. Like always, some accept it, and others reject it. Like the Bible says, "Everything is permissible but not everything is beneficial." I hope and pray that you have been blessed, and if not, at least challenged to seek the Lord while He may be found.

If you are finishing this book as a non-believer, then you need to place me in a category—liar, lunatic, or legitimate. This is too intense of a story to make up. This is about life and death—eternal life and eternal death. You may ask why the price that was paid for your soul was so incredibly high.

Well, I believe it was for two reasons. One, because sin has such a putrid and devastating effect on so many. It comes accompanied with a huge, gigantic, enormous cost. But the second reason the price was so high is because God wants you to know that you have great redemptive value to Him. In other words, you are so precious and valuable in His sight that He needed to place a priceless price tag on your soul, so no one could purchase you besides Him. He not only wanted the credit, but He wanted you to receive the revelation that He is absolutely and unequivocally crazy about you.

King David says in Psalm 113 that the Lord takes us from the ash heap to sitting with princes. The Lord wants to say to you, "There are different kingdoms: The kingdom of darkness and the Royal Kingdom of My Light. You are royalty. You have been robbed of your excellence. Let Me restore your excellence and teach you how to love."

I dare you; in fact, I double dare you to talk to God. Ask Him for yourself if I am a liar or a lunatic. The Lord is real and if you miss this truth, you miss out on the greatest and most amazing gift life has to offer you. As a physical trainer, my clients were of the upper echelons of society, for example a billionaire, an international model, as well as a Hollywood actress. I have been on their private learjets, cruised on their Italian yachts, spent time in the most exotic islands in the world, and have been to the best parties life can throw. I experienced the best life has to offer and I consider it dung compared to knowing God! If I added up all the greatest times I have ever had, it would not hold a candle to just one day with the Lord. King David states it so beautifully in Psalm 84, "Better is one day in your courts, Oh Lord, than a thousand days elsewhere."

If you will go out on a limb and ask, seek, and knock, I believe you too will get answers. You will find that doors will open that will lead you to the Ultimate Door, Yeshua (Jesus) Himself, which will be your very entry way into the Kingdom. Remember, you too can go from the ash heap to sitting with princes as King David did or from the projects to His palace as I have, and fall prey to His conspiracy of grace.

I pray that the Lord will bless you and keep you. I pray that the Lord will make His face shine upon you and be gracious to you. I pray that the Lord will lift up His countenance upon you and give you His peace, in the name of the Prince of all Peace, Yeshua. Amen!

Preaching to pastors in Kenya

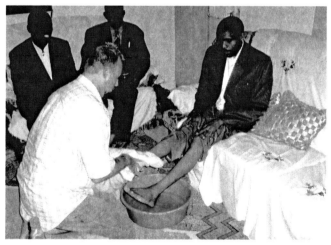

Washing the pastors' feet in Kenya

149

# CHAPTER TEN

# TRUE RICHES

Center: The Torah scroll, Menorah, and the "Ark" where the Torah scroll is stored in our synagogue

Outside: Stained glass windows of our synagogue representing the twelve tribes of Israel

To the right: The front entrance to our new synagogue featuring flora native to Israel

Can a person encounter Almighty God and stay the same? Here I am sitting in my office May 2011 and it is hard to believe that this kid from the projects is heading up an international ministry. My story really is from rags to riches to True Riches!

Please don't misunderstand me. I am not one to boast other than in the Lord, without whom I am doomed. I wish I could take the credit but I know myself all too well. To God be all the glory! Left to my own devices, well, perish the thought!

Let me give you a brief update. My family and I came to Macon, Georgia back in January 2003. We came to lead a rather small fellowship of Jews and Gentiles alike meeting in a storefront. Today we have a beautiful facility that has become our missions base for our international ministry.

I must tell you a little bit of the story. We came here and the congregational bank account was just about empty. Then the Lord began to make an impact and more and more folks came to see what was going on at this "Messianic Synagogue" where we worshipped with a Hebraic, first century flavor. We had liturgy, praise and worship, a plethora of Scripture, and the priestly blessing, of course.

Then the Lord prompted us in 2005 (just two years after I came) to purchase land for building a Messianic center in Macon, Georgia. We were a tad disobedient as we looked at buildings that were already built. It soon became very clear that the Lord wanted us to construct something from scratch. Well, we searched for land for months and there was not much to be had. The land that was available was either overpriced or in a locale that would just not work. With every search, the Lord would not give us the okay. So what do you do when you feel as though things aren't going well? You cry out to the Lord for direction. I did that and the Lord told me to fast for three days and He would let me know about the land we were to purchase. On the second day of the fast, my wife inquired if I had heard anything and I said that the Lord would tell me at the very end of the fast. It was the third day and I was excited to hear from God as well as get something to eat!

At the very end of the fast the Lord spoke and said "The price is right!" Well, the only thought in my mind lately had been, "The price is wrong!" We were looking at land that was way over our budget at $1 million an acre. We had all of $250,000 at the time. I do not personally believe in indebtedness so to me the price was very wrong.

So I spoke aloud. Well truth be told, I got real loud and I said, "Lord I don't get it." To which He said, "You sure don't, because I am not talking here about money but location." Interestingly enough I live off a short road about a mile long called none other than Price Road! I drive on this road four to five times every day, but I never dreamed that this could be our Congregation's future home. I looked and lo and behold there was one tract of land that was for sale. It was an old horse farm and it was twelve acres. All I could think of was the twelve tribes of Israel, the twelve apostles, as well as twelve being the number that represents the Lord's government, according to Gematria (Biblical numerology).

I still needed to know if this was "our" land or not. So I asked the Lord to give me a confirmation. He did. There was one horse stall still on the property. The Lord instructed me to walk over to that horse stall and look up over the entrance which bore a wooden sign. At the time, we were expecting our fourth child who after much prayer was to be named Lily. As I looked up, lo and behold the name on the wooden sign was none other than LILY! Hallelujah. Once again the Lord came through.

So we made an offer and it was accepted. Once again our bank account was zeroed out. Then the Lord told me to plan to build a facility. He told me that He was giving me a mandate not a mortgage. I told Him I had no idea about the design nor the plan of a building. He told me that He had the design and the plan, just like He had when the Hebrews built the Tabernacle back in Exodus 25. The Lord gave me faith to wait for His instructions. I knew the Lord doesn't change so if He told Moses He would tell Greg!

First the Lord told me to create twelve very large four foot by ten foot stained glass windows for the sanctuary depicting the twelve tribes of Israel. I thought, "Windows without a building?" Then again Noah had a boat without water, and Moses had water without a boat, so I did it!

Long story short, we have a beautiful worship center that cost almost $3 million including all furnishings and fixtures as well as a beautiful landscape which mimics all the flora of Israel. Oh, the best part is we have no mortgage! Praise God!

How did we do it? We didn't. He did! I don't have an edifice complex, but it is quite beautiful and depicts the beautiful majesty and awesomeness of our God.

Since then, in just seven short years, the Lord has done amazing things. We now have a Congregation in Nakuru, Kenya with a school and an orphanage called Congregation Beth Yeshua Kenya.

With orphans in Kenya

It is growing each and every day and the work God is doing is wonderful. The ministry there is far reaching into countries like Tanzania, Uganda, Rwanda, Burundi and the Congo.

The leader of Beth Yeshua Kenya, Stephen N'Ganga and his family

We also have a major network in India of over 150 Congregations with over 100 Pastors, growing and working under our ministry called Beth Yeshua India. We have seen over 10,000 people come to the fold in just five short years. This all started with an e-mail and 100 Bibles sent to just one little village fellowship.

Get this, Mate. We are currently under way to establish Congregation Beth Yeshua in the Gold Coast of Australia! Another very important outreach is in Israel. We are deeply involved with a major work there called Neve Michael where we provide for 30 children who have been through the mill, to say the least. We are also involved locally with ministries right here in our own backyard in Macon where we currently minister to over 40 inner-city children each and every week.

Who would have thought that coming to Macon, Georgia to lead a small Messianic Congregation with approximately forty people would turn into a global ministry reaching to the far ends of the earth through online streaming and internet radio? God has done an amazing work. As I write, I am humbled that the Lord has been so gracious to me. I sometimes ask my wife why He has. All she says is, "Because you're willing."

I have to tell you I just love the Lord. I mean I am crazy about Him. To think that He is my inheritance is great. I am more than satisfied with Him. But to think that I am His inheritance is clearly over the top. "You mean to say, Rabbi, that we are all He wants?" Once again the Lord wants none to perish, and He takes no delight nor does He receive any pleasure when one dies in their sins. Please consider all you have read and receive all the Lord has for you. For you too can go from the projects to His palace!!!

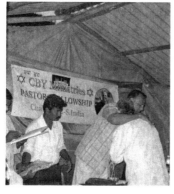

157

Notice the Israeli flag.

Synagogue and School
in India built by
Beth Yeshua
International

Worship
services in India

Women from the
Lambada Tribe

159

This book is available at:

**olivepresspublisher.com**

**amazon.com**

**barnesandnoble.com**

and other websites.

The E-book is available at:

**amazon.com**

Book stores and distributors:
Obtain this book through:

**Ingram Book Company**

To schedule  the author for
a speaking  engagement
or conference:

E-mail: **admin@bethyeshua.com**

Phone: **478-471-9955**


To learn more about the author's
current ministry:

Website: **www.bethyeshua.com**

CPSIA information can be obtained at www.ICGtesting.com
Printed in the USA
LVOW130008230712

291101LV00005B/1/P